Every Wolf's Howl

Barry Grills

A memoir

Canada Council for the Arts Conseil des Arts du Canada

Freehand Books gratefully acknowledges the support of the Canada Council for the Arts for its publishing program. ¶ Freehand Books, an imprint of Broadview Press Inc., acknowledges the financial support for its publishing program provided by the Government of Canada through the Canada Book Fund.

Freehand Books
515 - 815 1st Street SW Calgary, Alberta T2P 1N3
www.freehand-books.com

Book orders: LitDistCo
100 Armstrong Avenue Georgetown, Ontario L7G 5S4
Telephone: 1-800-591-6250 Fax: 1-800-591-6251
orders@litdistco.ca
www.litdistco.ca

Library and Archives Canada Cataloguing In Publication

Grills, Barry

Every wolf's howl / Barry Grills.

ISBN 978-1-55481-105-2

1. German shepherd dog—Canada—Biography. 2. Human-animal relationships—Canada—Biography. 3. Grills, Barry. 4. Grills, Barry—Health. 5. Dog owners—Canada—Biography. 6. Newspapers—Ownership—Biography. I. Title.

SF429.G37G75 2012 636.737'6 C2012-904883-6

Edited by Robyn Read
Book design and cover illustration by Natalie Olsen, kisscutdesign.com
Author photo by Liz Lott

Printed on FSC recycled paper and bound in Canada

Every Wolf's Howl

In memory of Lupus

Every wolf's and lion's howl

Raises from hell a human soul.

WILLIAM BLAKE

"Auguries of Innocence"

Preface

Most of what follows is true. A little of it is invention. I believe we construct the narrative of our lives out of an amalgam of fact and fiction; memory manipulates events to fit the pattern of our perceptions, and the objective truth of the things that happen to us is filtered through our subjective interpretations. We order our lives like stories to give them form and allow ourselves to make some kind of sense out of them.

Most of the events in this book happened the way they're described. A few of them probably didn't. I have taken some liberties with omissions or shortcuts. There was an actual Lupus, an actual Mingus. There are and were the people who appear so anonymously in this book. And all of us continue to live within the same ambiguous society, a society negotiating various ideological detours on the way towards some kind of purposeful civilization.

Our lives ramble much more than stories. And this is just a story.

Pretty much all of it happened, though. A little of it probably didn't.

April 1996

It's April—the nineteenth, I think. A calendar is pinned to the wall above my desk: wolves in various poses and wilderness settings, a Christmas gift. I look at the pictures frequently, the grid of numbered days hardly at all. My days have structure even if they aren't named or numbered. They still happen. When they're anonymous, I prefer them. This is something I've learned to appreciate relatively late in life.

These days Lupus is the main reason I live by any kind of schedule at all. It's ironic, really: I used to have little else but routine, Lupus was responsible for breaking me of it; and now his routine is the one that remains, the one we share. His first walk of the day is around nine in the morning, therefore so is mine.

His second is shortly after seven p.m. So is mine. During the day we find other activities to occupy our time, going to town, perhaps, or locating a trail in the woods. Exploring, discovering.

I've been told that we're attached at the hip. His choice; he's trained me very well. In our early days together, I tried on several occasions to leave him at home alone for a few hours, but he so thoroughly punished me for it I soon gave up. He gnawed on doorjambs, turned over small tables, moved various items around, and generally created a terrible mess. Once he jumped onto my bed and, calibrating an area exactly in the centre, urinated on it. I discovered his objections as I was retiring for the night. Now, for those infrequent circumstances when I cannot take him with me, I have a friend come by to sit with him. He does no damage as long as someone is around, although he conveys his discontent by refusing to remain in the same room as his sitter. As soon as his sitter enters a room, he leaves to find another spot in which to sulk. I'm told he is inconsolable in my absence.

When we go to the city, he'll wait for me in the car, but his time limit is two hours. Any longer than this and there will be reprisals. One February afternoon a couple of years ago, I got held up at a meeting, and he tried to eat my car. He shredded the padding around the windows and doors, the steering wheel, and the knob on the gearshift between the two front seats. He pried the doorjamb apart on the driver's side. Once I got over my initial shock at the extent of the damage, I realized I was more annoyed at the lengthy nonproductivity of the meeting than I was with Lupus. And the duct tape I used to repair what I could of the damage matched the colour of the car's interior. This made it easier to forgive him.

We were boarding in Kingston at the time. When I pulled up in the car to my parking space behind the house, my landlord approached to inspect the damage; he seemed more disgusted with what Lupus had done than I could ever have been. "I wouldn't have a dog like that," he'd said. "If I had a dog that did that . . ."

"I'll live with it," I said.

". . . I'd put him down for it."

I gazed at him for a moment, his true nature passing in critical review before my eyes. "It's just a fucking car," I said and turned away.

I no longer live in Kingston. Now Lupus and I live half an hour north of there. We have new rituals, new habits, new freedoms. I now believe I know what in life to ignore. Lupus taught me what is important; he teaches me still.

It's morning and I'm standing at the sliding glass doors that face the backyard, sipping coffee and trying to get a fix on the weather. It's been raining. The chill and dampness have found their way inside. Outdoors, I know, I'll see my breath, a more modest version of the mist drifting off the lawn and weaving itself through the barren, arthritic fingers of the maples at the end of the garden. Spring is a little late arriving; today's colours are various forlorn hues of brown and grey against a sky so impenetrable with cloud I feel crushed beneath it.

"Not a nice day, Loop," I observe. Most days begin with a remark about the weather.

He lifts his head to glance at me from his place on the carpeted floor by my bed. At least, without looking at him, this is what I assume he does. After three and a half years together, certain responses have become habitual, but perhaps on this particular morning Lupus doesn't budge, preferring to remain by my bed in a ball, his nose covered by his bushy tail, in a position I call his *husky curl*.

I sip my coffee, gazing out at the back garden. Waiting, I suppose.

Waiting, Lupus dozes.

I can hear my landlady's boyfriend on the other side of the door that separates my apartment from the rest of the house. I rent two small rooms in this house, a bedroom and a living area that I've converted into an office. My quarters are separated from the kitchen, which I share with my landlady, by a pair of wooden accordion doors. My landlady recently installed a new airtight stove in her kitchen, and after a while I detect the sounds of her boyfriend building a fire. The boyfriend is also relatively new. He's an engineer and he's good with fires. Last winter, before the new boyfriend and the new airtight stove, I would have gone into the kitchen myself to build a fire in my landlady's cookstove. Sagittarian in the Year of the Rat. I'm told we start the morning fires, tuck people in for the night, and check the locks at the end of the day. After lighting the fire, I would have crept upstairs to the bathroom to relieve myself, careful not to disturb my landlady who rises later than I do. These days I piss into a large plastic Pepsi bottle that I keep at the foot of my bed. I'll take it upstairs to empty and clean it after my landlady and her boyfriend have left for the day.

My landlady's boyfriend poked a hole about a foot square in the wall of my apartment to give me more heat from the new stove. But the conduit doesn't allow enough heat to penetrate; my floor remains cold and I have to open the slatted accordion doors to share in some of the warmth. In this way, I intrude on my landlady's life, and she intrudes on mine.

I pour myself more coffee. The coffeemaker is mine, it didn't come with the place. My landlady doesn't drink coffee or eat red meat; her body is a temple. Her boyfriend doesn't drink coffee either; he's on government disability, clinically depressed since he lost his job a couple of years ago, and he says it makes him anxious. I drink a lot of coffee. As I approach the end of my forties, I've decided my body is *not* a temple. No, scarred by time and abuse, it's happy to be alive.

My landlady's boyfriend climbs the creaking stairs back to the bedroom to lie under the covers until the house heats up. He only comes to stay a couple of nights each week.

My landlady doesn't like it if the people in the village assume that she and I are an item. She maintains that she is shy. Back when we were getting to know one another, when I first moved in, we debated shyness philosophically. She suggested that her shyness reflects an admirable humility. I countered that shyness is predicated upon the notion of walking into a room of strangers and wondering what people will think of you—a self-absorbed preoccupation. The idea, I said, is to walk into a room and wonder what you will think of everybody else.

Based on this alone—one pair of a dozen irreconcilable opinions—we could never have been an item, even if we'd wanted to be. Not the point, though. Just as long as we don't appear to be one to our neighbours in this tiny hamlet. She explains whenever she can and to whomever will listen that our arrangement is strictly business. I provide the same explanation, respecting her wishes, whenever someone refers to her as something other than my landlady.

On the way to pour myself a third mug of coffee, I bend to pat Lupus on the head. I cannot resist him; I am human and must touch. He accepts affection without display, which I attribute to his lupine heritage. Lupus is a German shepherd cross, more wolf than dog, I've discovered. The dog in him wants to roll over on its back and have its belly rubbed, but the aloof wolf side controls his behaviour most of the time. *Pet me if you must, but don't think that I enjoy it.* I've come to believe that accepting affection with tolerance is his way of giving affection back.

This morning I am newly but cautiously in love, and the rituals between Lupus and me have begun to change. Our daily routines now have to make room for an additional human and canine. We no longer live quite so privately. My new girlfriend has an Alaskan malamute-German shepherd named Mingus. We met through our dogs more than three months ago. The two animals were attracted to one another from the beginning, and now they behave like siblings.

Together Lupus and Mingus are a striking pair. They are both shockingly handsome and seem to know it. On their leashes, they strut down the street, heads held high, tugging us along in their wake.

Mingus is a good host whenever we visit my girlfriend's home. He entertains his friend, leading him around the house, showing him which doors to push open, which windows provide a view to the outside. Lupus isn't a good host at all. When Mingus visits, he lies down in his spot by my bed, making it clear that Mingus is responsible for his own amusement, which usually consists of paying too much attention to Charlie, my landlady's cat. Mingus hates cats with a passion Lupus doesn't share. Dog and wolf-dog can seem so similar; but there will always be times they demonstrate how very different they are.

And yet, Lupus is learning from Mingus. Lately, after I've left him with my girlfriend for an hour or two, Lupus has come to the door to greet me with affection when I return, something he's never done before. He does this, I realize, because Mingus does this. Whenever I appear at the door, Mingus cries and wags his tail and brings me a toy in his mouth. Feeling left out, Lupus has begun to share in the regular celebration of my return. Perhaps soon he'll learn to wag his tail in welcome, the way Mingus does, rather than reserving his tail-wagging only for those times when he's up to no good. Maybe Lupus will learn to bark from Mingus, in much the same way he's teaching Mingus to howl. I look forward to this with more than a passing interest.

Lupus cannot bark beyond a whisper. Sometimes at night he'll hear something outside and want, for a moment, to behave like a watchdog. He woofs. But it comes out so quietly that I'm embarrassed for both of us. The whispered bark doesn't mean he has nothing to say, only that barking isn't his language. No, Lupus speaks by howling, *howling* is his language. I've learned he's happier with himself when he remembers this, when he remembers what he is.

Most of the time he's silent, but when he gets going, his

cries develop into a conversation, especially if I answer back. On the nights that I drive to the city for a coffee with friends, when I return to the car after an hour or so, he complains about being left behind. As I walk to the hatchback, I know he's upset if I discover he's abandoned the blanket in the back to sit impatiently behind the wheel. As I climb in, he moves to the other bucket seat, sits, and begins to howl, partially in greeting, partially to get my goat. Soon we are acting out a good-natured imitatively spousal scene, in which I must justify my occasional need to associate with my fellow human beings in places where he isn't welcome.

"Ooh-woooh," he complains as we drive away, his nose tilted nearly to the ceiling.

"C'mon now, Loop," I counter. "You know I have to — "

"Ooh-woooh."

" — get out on my own now and then."

And so it goes, as we drive down the city streets towards the highway that will take us home. A playful argument. Our protests drifting out the windows and upwards into the night sky, both of us howling, arguing, and laughing, enjoying the humour in this improbable set of circumstances, the two of us speaking just to hear what the other says.

What exists between us is more than mere friendship. Lupus has accompanied me through a couple of years of drastic change, and now he keeps me from going back to where I was during those years, a time when I viewed the future with a mixture of uncertainty and dread.

I pour myself a final half mug of coffee and turn the coffeemaker off. I return to the sliding doors and ponder the grey-brown pout of the day on the other side of the glass. As I finish my coffee, Lupus gets to his feet, ready for his morning walk. I suspect he knows when it's time by counting the number of mugs of coffee I've drunk.

I put on my winter coat and decide to wear my gloves. I put a fluorescent green tennis ball in my pocket and, having attached Lupus to his leash, pass through the accordion doors into the kitchen. The living room is now warm from the heat of the stove. My landlady and her boyfriend have crept downstairs. They sit in silence on the couch, close to one another, engaged in a whispered discussion of one of the complex relationship issues they seem to sort through endlessly. She wants children and he doesn't; he gets increasingly depressed about being out of work; the world is watching them and, as always, judging them. Sometimes I think my landlady enjoys playing the role of mother to her younger boyfriend, who in turn is happy to play the role of her son.

"Good morning," I say cheerfully enough.

The boyfriend nods.

"Going for your walk?" my landlady asks.

"Down to the park," I say, "for a half hour or so."

It won't be long enough for them to settle anything, but at least they can raise their voices while I'm not in the house.

I glance at her engineer.

"Have a good one," he suggests.

The village of Yarker isn't much. A river divides it into two equal halves and there's a noisy waterfall in the heart of town. The waterfall is invisible from the rusty steel bridge we cross on the way to the park, but we can hear the endless roar and glimpse the dancing mist. There are only two stores in town. One is a junk store advertising antiques. The other is a general store selling food so overpriced I cannot afford it. But I rent videos there sometimes; it has a wide selection. Clustered around this humble business section are houses new and old, well-kept and rundown, shuffled together like two unmatched decks of cards.

Lupus takes the lead, and our route never varies. For him activities such as this must be ritual in every way. He tugs stubbornly on the leash as we make our way along the sidewalk towards the general store, which also functions as the village post office. The driver of the mail van sometimes gives him two large dog biscuits. Lupus knows the mailman's truck, and he anticipates the treat in advance. The nature of our walk tends to be defined by whether Lupus receives the biscuits on the way to the park or on the way back. If we pick them up on the way to the park, he carries one in his mouth and I put the other in my pocket. When we arrive at the park, he buries his biscuit so that he can enjoy his play unimpeded; I must memorize where he puts it so that I can clandestinely dig it up when we are done. If he catches me at this before it's time to leave, he'll only ask for the biscuit and bury it again. If he's given the biscuits on our way back home, he carries one with him and whines for the duration of the walk, only stopping when we reach our destination and he can safely devour his treat. If we miss the driver altogether, he leaves the two biscuits just under a metal railing on the store's concrete steps. No truck this morning, and no biscuits, so Lupus stops hurrying me along. When we reach the bridge, he sticks his head through the metal grill to peer into the mist of the waterfall. He does this each morning like he's taking inventory. When he's satisfied, we continue the rest of the way across the bridge.

I enjoy this walk every day, even if it's raining or snowing. I talk to Lupus as we hurry along, and he listens to what I have to say. He's good on a leash, for a lupine cross. If he wanted to, he could drag me down the street. But we've walked thousands of miles together and know each other well.

We pass seven or eight houses, then follow a bend in the road near the community hall. Around the bend, the park, our usual destination, presents itself. The grass, still brown and humble from winter, is wet with last night's rain. Beads of moisture gather sadly on rusting playground equipment.

I reach down and release Lupus's leash. He dashes to the edge of the river and stands on its bank, gazing hatefully at three ducks and a large goose that are treading water several yards from shore. He taunts them silently from where he stands, like some officious border guard daring them to trespass on his territory.

Lupus isn't really interested in the ducks; his true nemesis is the goose. They share so much enmity there is no hope of alliance or reconciliation. A couple of times last summer, Lupus and I happened to encounter the goose while it was strutting along the shore. On each occasion, Lupus chased it fluttering and honking back into the river, then turned to me for approval. When Lupus is feeling cocky, he often glances at me to make sure I'm suitably impressed by whatever display of prowess he has just executed. Then, one day last fall, as Lupus stood on the shore, the goose charged across the water, finally insulted enough to want to take him on. Lupus held his ground, glancing back at me with a bemused look. "Doesn't that damn bird know I'm a wolf?" his expression implied. The goose, realizing Lupus wasn't going to run, succumbed to a change of heart just before it reached the shore, braking and honking loudly. Its bluff called, it retreated back to the centre of the stream.

Today goose and wolf-dog avoid any altercation, and Lupus soon loses interest in the waterfowl. He asks me to throw the tennis ball, wagging his tail in entreaty while I fish it out of my pocket. I toss the ball deep into the park, then stand there watching him play. With Lupus I need throw the ball only once. After that he throws it for himself, chasing it in silence, catching it on the third or fourth bounce and snapping his head around to toss it again. The silence makes his game eerie. He gives no growl, no bark, not even a snort. He hunts this way as well, in silent earnestness.

When he tires of the ball, he leaves it on the ground, often in some faraway point in the park and I must go and pick it up. If I ask him to bring me the ball, he only looks at me in disgust. As a self-appointed aristocrat, there are things he just won't do.

I stand in the morning gloom with the leash around my neck while Lupus, finished with the ball, checks his territory. I think about my girlfriend and Mingus. Lupus and I will visit them tomorrow. Tomorrow my girlfriend and I will continue down a path leading somewhere desperately hopeful. I glance at Lupus, now several yards away from me. He staggers a bit, recovers, and heads in my direction. Then he staggers again, profoundly this time. His legs buckle, and he falls to the ground.

"Loop?"

I race towards him. He lies on his side, panting. His eyes are glazed. I crouch down and touch the damp fur of his shoulder. "Loop? Are you all right?" He whines piteously. "Loop? C'mon now, get up. Get up, Loop." I'm helpless in my desperation. He whines once more, falls silent, and stops breathing. "Loop, c'mon," I cry. "What's the matter with you? You're okay, big fella."

But I know he's not okay. It's just that I want this moment to be a terrible mistake.

I must get him to the vet. I run out of the park and back through the town, desperate to reach my car. Lupus's leash is still coiled around my neck; it thumps against my chest as I run. As I pass the general store, I notice two dog biscuits on the concrete steps. The poignancy of the two biscuits sitting there sends me into a frenzy. I start asking myself frantic questions that don't make sense: What if he's not there when I get back with the car? What if someone steals him? I feel a little insane. I feel like I've been hit by lightning and am dancing in the electrical shock. I feel like I am dreaming and will never again wake up.

—

My landlady and her boyfriend, dazed by my breathless report that something may be wrong with Lupus, decide to accompany me back to the park. I know they both harbour deep affection for Lupus. Even on those occasions when I've been hard to like, Lupus has never fallen out of favour.

We take two cars. My landlady knows the complicated

network of back roads that lead to the vet's office because she's taken Charlie there a couple of times before.

I still believe I've made some kind of mistake, that when I return to the park Lupus will be sitting there wondering where the hell I've been. Like Lazarus, but with much more attitude. But he's still lying on the grass when we get there. Everything is painfully the same as it was when I left, a sameness exaggerated by the stillness of the day and its unreality. Even from a distance, I can see that Lupus is not breathing, and I'm angry at him for this. How dare he tear a hole in the canvas of what should have been just another ordinary day, the kind we've come to appreciate for its freedom and timelessness.

Guiltily, feeling I've abandoned him somehow, I touch his fur—the white, silver, and black of it—to make amends. It's beaded with moisture, as if nature's elements are already conspiring to dissolve what he once was.

My landlady's mournful voice sounds from somewhere behind my left shoulder: "Oh, Loop."

I retrieve the blanket from the back of my hatchback. The three of us spread it out and drag Lupus onto it, bending in tandem to pick it up so we can carry him to my car. Lupus was sixty pounds when last I weighed him. He seems heavier than that now.

My landlady rides along in my car, giving me directions down each dirt road. I know I would never be able to find the veterinary on my own, especially under circumstances such as these, so distraught am I with sadness and incredulity. The boyfriend follows at a discreet distance, well back from the flying gravel churned up by my rear tires. I keep looking at Lupus in the rear-view mirror, expecting somehow that he will suddenly sit up, blocking my view of the car's back window the way he has hundreds of times before. I'm used to hoping good things will happen, but today all hope seems strangely empty and irrelevant. I am aware now of the desperation that comes from a loss of faith.

I want to cry. But I've decided that crying would feel like giving up, like admitting this day has truly defeated me, transforming the man I thought I was earlier this morning into nothing but a hoax.

—

We carry him to a chrome table in an examination room. We lay him there and carefully remove the blanket.

The vet is a tall, awkward man who keeps nervously repositioning his eyeglasses. I suspect he's more comfortable with animals than he has ever been with people. I tell him what happened.

He nods as I explain, fiddling with his glasses, gazing thoughtfully at Lupus as though he will verify my story. "A beautiful animal," the vet remarks when I am done.

"Yes," I croak.

"Good shape."

"Yes, lots of exercise." Like I'm pleading my case.

"How old is he?"

"Five in the summer."

The veterinarian shakes his head. "Lot of wolf in there," he says. "I don't know," he adds, not explaining his doubt, whatever it might be.

I wonder how much longer I can prevent myself from crying.

I feel my throat seizing up, as if someone were stepping on it, crushing my voice, strangling the life out of me. "I just don't understand what happened to him," I manage to say. "He's been healthy ever since I've had him."

"I'd have to do an autopsy."

I ask him how much an autopsy costs. Lupus and I live a great distance below the poverty line, cherishing a kind of dignity there. Food, rent, and hope are all the luxuries we can afford.

When the vet answers me I don't actually hear his reply. But I'm too embarrassed to ask him to repeat himself and, besides, whatever the response, I'm sure the autopsy bill is beyond my means.

"Okay," I tell him.

I wonder how I'll find the money, but I must know what malevolent force murdered my best friend.

The vet goes into another room to get some paperwork for me to fill out. Then, unable to resist any longer, I burst into tears. After a brief hesitation, my landlady and her boyfriend take me into an awkward, three-cornered embrace. We stand there clumsily, holding on to one another while I sob like a baby, each of us succumbing to feelings of mingled grief and awkwardness.

But at last I'm willing to accept that it's true. Lupus is dead. Unquestionably, unequivocally, definitely, undeniably. That's death for you: a long list of adverbs, each one finite, each one connoting a state beyond the limitations of my futile grasp.

Back home I sit in my chair, and when I glance at my watch I'm surprised that it's not yet eleven o'clock. I feel like several hours have passed, even an entire arduous day. In a daze, I try to accomplish things, listlessly shuffling some papers around on my desk. I even remember to take the Pepsi bottle upstairs to empty and clean. Then, giving up, I sit down helplessly again, trying to accept the fact that Lupus is no longer lying here on the floor by the side of my bed.

The sameness numbs me. This place, these rooms, the day. Only Lupus is different. His absence is the crucial difference that renders everything he touched, especially me, different too. I feel angry with him for leaving me this way, as though his dying were a particularly selfish act.

At least I'm no longer confused. My mind no longer clings to some desperate, irrational hope. I know that Lupus is dead. I've begun to believe it.

But Charlie, my landlady's cat, doesn't understand. He comes and goes through my open door, clearly wondering where Lupus is. At one point, he hunkers down over Lupus's uneaten breakfast, knowing this should entice Lupus out of his hiding place. But Lupus doesn't appear, and Charlie, not really hungry, doesn't eat anything. Confused, Charlie goes away. Confused, Charlie soon comes back.

In the past, Charlie would sometimes covet Lupus's breakfast. He materialized some mornings after Lupus finished eating, intent on making a snack of the remaining food. Lupus would stroll to the scene of the impending crime and stand over the encroaching cat. Sometimes this was enough, and Charlie would flee. If he didn't, Lupus would bend down and, using his nose, gently push Charlie out the door. The eviction was so delicately achieved, no one was ever hurt. In a tolerant way they were friends and this dispute was only ceremonial.

When Lupus and I first moved in, there were a couple of rocky moments. Lupus, always curious, bent down to sniff Charlie, who lashed out with his claws, trying to nick Lupus on the nose. But Lupus was too fast. Cocky, enjoying the game, he kept his nose in close, tempting Charlie to hit it, ducking each attempt with an astonishing dexterity, smug and capable. Finally, grasping the hopelessness of it, Charlie dashed away from the scene of his embarrassment.

Lupus possessed extraordinary quickness. He proved it the January before last, when I was out chopping wood. It was a sunny, bitterly cold afternoon and Lupus had found a spot where he could sleep in the sunshine near the vicinity of my labours. At some point, as I grew tired, the maul I was using came down crookedly on a massive piece of wood I was splitting, and a large chunk propelled itself directly at him. I didn't have time to call an alarm, it happened too quickly. I only had time to catch a glimpse of the projectile hurtling towards its slumbering victim. But Lupus was gone before the piece of wood hit the ground. Although it struck the exact spot where he'd been sleeping, he was already six feet away, gazing back at the place where he had lain. He seemed invulnerable that day, gifted at survival.

Recalling his speed and strength makes me weep again. I get up and close my door to shut Charlie out. His confusion saddens me.

I hurt. I feel like I am drifting down some wet and chilly sluice. For more than three years, Lupus has been my intimate companion, my helper through a necessary transformation from sickness into health, from impatience into patience, and from confusion into a comfortable reconciliation between my previous self and some more realistic version of who I truly am. He was there each time I was betrayed along the way, and each time I accepted the betrayal. I feel vaguely afraid to carry on without him. How will I keep healing myself without Lupus to inspire me?

Sitting here, drowning in grief, I fear I will forget everything I've learned. I will slide backwards and become the person I was when Lupus and I first met: a strange, guilty, driven man, terrified of failure. I am even afraid I will never be articulate enough to explain the nature of today's loss, to myself or to anyone else. I am afraid I will stagger around too long, searching for the light that illuminates the end of a period of pain, forced to accept that I am now permanently blind.

Eventually I reach for the telephone and begin to call the people who should be informed, the people who love Lupus and sometimes care for us both.

"Oh no," my father says, his voice cracking at the news.

Lupus has long since been forgiven for the time he stepped in the flower garden in front of my parents' home. He so terrorized the squirrels in their backyard, my father would forgive him anything.

"I'm sorry," he says now.

"I'm sorry too," my mother adds.

When I telephone my friends, a couple of them suggest that I should cremate his remains because Lupus was so special, and our bond was so deep. But I demur. I don't even know how I will pay for the autopsy. They offer to help me with this expense, offer to lend me money. Gratefully, I accept. But I'm ashamed to admit to them that I don't know when I can pay it back.

At last I call my girlfriend. Just hearing her say, "Hello," makes me weep again.

"It's Lupus," I say around the ache in my throat. "Lupus died this morning."

It's nearly one o'clock by the time I get to Kingston. I find my girlfriend's house without noticing the route along the way. One moment I am on the highway heading south, the next I'm pulling up in front of her door.

My girlfriend is waiting for me; she opens the door before I knock. I collapse into her embrace, weeping again.

"It's okay," she keeps saying. "It's okay."

Like Charlie, Mingus doesn't understand. When my girlfriend and I sit down on the couch, he goes to the living room window to peer outside at my car. As far as he knows, Lupus should be here. He looks from me to the window and back again, complaining quietly with whines and little groans.

"I'm sorry, Mingus," I say. "Lupus won't be coming here anymore."

He gazes at me a moment, considering what I've said, understanding the sadness in my voice if not my spoken words. Then, astonishingly, he comes to me and climbs up on my lap, his forelegs on my chest, his back legs on the floor. He buries his head against my neck and whines. At more than seventy pounds, he's bigger than Lupus, but I let him rest against me because he too needs to mourn.

Shortly, after Mingus has found a spot to lie down where he can keep an eye on us, my girlfriend explains she's traded shifts with a friend so that she can be with me today.

I thank her for her understanding. My girlfriend is a crisis counsellor. When she says she understands, I know it is true.

I get through that first day somehow. I keep plummeting into snakepits of sadness, and I feel grateful every time I arduously climb out again. I tell anecdotes about Lupus almost ceaselessly. Although the pain is agonizing, I'm compelled to talk about him, as if by talking about him I can retain my hold on whatever is left of him.

In some ways, here with my girlfriend and Mingus, it's harder to believe he's gone. Only a few days ago, we took Lupus and Mingus for a drive with us. I remember both dogs standing like elegant centurions in the back of my car, their heads protruding over the seats to take in all the sights. Only a couple of days before that, we took them to Victoria Park, not far from my girlfriend's house, where they played with the other dogs who gather there, the two of them taking charge of the pack the way they always did. When they needed a rest, Lupus would come and sit by my leg, where he'd break into an exuberant howl. Mingus's cries would follow instantly. In a second or two, the entire group would start up, and those of us gathered there would dissolve into laughter at this incomprehensible cacophony.

And it was only nineteen days ago that Mingus's master and I departed the safety of platonic friendship for the risky territory we explore as lovers.

Now she helps me through this day and night. There are gaps in my grief—a couple of times when we make love, a few vaguely hopeful conversations—wedged between recurring periods of anger, loss, and sadness.

I decide to cremate Lupus, after all. I call the vet to arrange for the retrieval of Lupus's body. The autopsy, I am told, revealed that he died of a massive heart attack.

"Everything just exploded," is how the veterinarian describes it.

"He wasn't poisoned or anything, was he?"

"No. It must have been congenital," he says.

"I just wanted to make sure no one was to blame."

He doesn't remark on this.

I stay with Mingus and my girlfriend for two days and two nights, craving consolation. Then she must go back to work and I must return home, to get Lupus's remains and begin discovering the resources to be normal again. The weather warms up, as if spring has no respect for the gloom that is reflective of my grief.

I retrieve Lupus's body, which the vet has placed in a sturdy plastic bag, and put it in the shed at the bottom of my landlady's garden until I can take it to be cremated the next day. By this time his body is beginning to rot, on account of the warm days that have passed since his death. I must keep the hatchback windows down to make the long journey with him to dispose of his remains. The stench is not unbearable, only achingly sad. That the joy of life should come to this: a state of putrid decay.

There is no ceremony of closure. I'm not sure there ever is with death. When we arrive at the veterinary where Lupus is to be cremated, I carry his carcass around back and leave it on a loading ramp. I am breathing cautiously. I'm to pick up his ashes a few days later.

I apologize that he's begun to smell, and that his chain is still around his neck.

"Will you be wanting it back?" The man at the loading ramp wants to know.

"The ashes?" I reply in surprise.

"No, the chain."

"Oh, no," I say. "I won't be needing it. I think of it as his."

And I do. The chain that served as his collar was made for a much larger animal. Its two predecessors, marginally less thick, had to be replaced because Lupus was so strong he could bend the heavy eyelets at either end of the chain. This recollection brings on a renewed sadness. Lupus's strength continues to be a reminder of the unexpectedness, the prematurity of his death.

Back home his absence is everywhere. When I sit down to a meal, I find that I keep my feet tucked under my chair in case, in stretching out, I might inadvertently kick the animal that is no longer lying there. I'm careful climbing out of bed in the morning for fear I'll step on him. I empty his dishes, clean them, and put them in a bag to give to Mingus. I believe Lupus would approve.

Charlie spends several more days wondering why Lupus isn't here. Sometimes when I'm eating, he peers around the doorjamb between the kitchen and the living room, as puzzled as I am that Lupus isn't lying under the kitchen table. I wonder if he remembers the time he stole into the kitchen, lusting after a plate of roast chicken I had placed on the freezer lid. He stood at the front of the freezer, flexing his muscles to leap up and steal some food from me, but before he was able to make his move, Lupus howled the alarm. Caught, Charlie dashed into the living room. I wonder if he remembers Lupus positioning himself between the freezer and the doorway, so that when Charlie peered cautiously around the corner, he came face to face with Lupus, who stood dutifully on guard.

I don't know what animals remember.

Somehow I find the strength to write my former partner about Lupus's death. She is in Central America again, reintroducing herself to dangers I do not understand. "We've lost our beloved Lupus," is how I begin. Regardless of how our relationship collapsed, of who was to blame or why, of the punishments we have each endured separately since, I know that she loved Lupus and must be told that he is gone.

The next day, I pick up Lupus's ashes. They are in a small cardboard carton, the kind that usually contains Chinese take-out rice. His name is scrawled in a corner on the top. I find a place for his ashes on a bookshelf, not yet knowing what kind of more permanent container I'll want to keep them in. I expect that at some point down the road I'll want to scatter them in the woods somewhere, because he was happiest when we were hiking the wilderness. But not yet. I can't let go yet. I'm afraid that when his ashes are gone, we'll be separated completely, and I'll lose the half of myself that Lupus helped me to prefer.

At times during this period of mourning, as I sit in the kitchen after my evening meal, my landlady comes in to ask me if I'm all right.

"Oh, sure," I usually say. "It just takes time, that's all."

She accepts my remark gingerly. Still, I feel a tension, a

trepidation in her demeanour that I do not understand. Then, one day towards the end of April, she comes to me and asks me to leave. She says, although the rent I pay has been useful, that she wants to live in her house alone.

I remind her that it was her idea to have me board with her in the first place. But she's concerned that Mingus, without Lupus to intercede, will hurt Charlie when he and my girlfriend come to visit. "I've been thinking about that," I reply. "It's best I visit them. They don't *have* to come here, you know."

"No, that isn't fair. Besides, I want to live here alone."

"I see."

"Things have changed," she adds.

I arrange to be gone by the end of June.

"I know this isn't the best time," she admits. "You know, with Lupus gone and everything."

"No," I tell her. "It's not."

But she sets her mouth firmly and stands in front of me, trying to make some point I do not understand.

"I'll survive," I say.

December 1995

I meet the woman who will become my girlfriend on a blustery December day in Kingston's Victoria Park, a place I sometimes take Lupus to renew his companionship with other dogs. Lupus and Mingus meet first. They are not as reserved as human beings tend to be these days. They don't fret about the risk involved in getting to know a stranger.

It's cold and a winter storm has dumped half a foot of snow on the ground. The sky remains cloudy, and it feels like more snow might fall. I think of today as winter-arrogant, exuding a needless bluster, as if the storm it contrived yesterday didn't quite make its point. I wear a scarf and toque, but a nasty little wind still finds a way to slap my cheeks.

I am feeling quite mortal this morning, a hangover from feeling terribly mortal the previous day. Yesterday I flew out of Halifax rollercoaster-style, the plane buffeted by a bitter, sullen wind off the Atlantic. I had been in Nova Scotia finishing off some research for a book I've been contracted to write, a biography about the life of Anne Murray. The captain apologized over the PA system for the bumpy takeoff. "This is Halifax in winter," he announced drolly.

However, the pilot on the rocky connecting flight from Toronto to Kingston felt no need to apologize for the violent weather. As the small plane negotiated its way through the Ontario storm, I appeared to suffer my apprehension alone. No one else seemed to mind: their eyes remained focused on newspaper business reports, the rising and falling stock prices.

Today, though, everything is back to normal. Once again I am safe but poor. I am on the ground with Lupus and the magical mystery of being away — all expenses paid — is already drifting into a surreal corner of my past.

Lupus and I like Victoria Park. It's spacious, and it provides him with an opportunity to play with other dogs gathered here. About a dozen people bring their dogs to this park regularly. I doubt any of us would come here were it not for this chance for our dogs to socialize while we stand by clutching leashes, and toys, balls, and sticks, chatting anonymously.

We rarely exchange names ourselves, although we introduce our dogs. "Here comes Lupus," someone usually says as we enter the park. We're all dog lovers here. Our occupations or family trees are irrelevant. We are here to expand our dogs' worlds; it doesn't matter if our own remain shrunken. We are so devoted to our dogs that we happily pay the price of gathering as humans who have no interest in one another.

In my mind, it is the times, the proclivity for poverty and uncertainty, that are responsible for this emotional disconnection. People don't make any attempt to know one another anymore. The less people invest in one another, whether tangibly or emotionally, the less can be taken away. Trust, even camaraderie, feels like risky business.

There are four or five of us in the park today. Our dogs finish their sniffing around and run from place to place, chasing sticks or each other. I've learned in recent years that there are two kinds of dogs. Some prefer to play with their masters rather than with members of their own species. Others relish the opportunity to ignore their human masters for a precious half hour or so, reacquainting themselves with some distantly remembered commune that used to be the pack. Lupus is one of these. As it turns out, so is Mingus.

They meet the very moment Mingus dashes into the park. They sniff at each other, then draw away, then follow one another from one urine-spotted snowbank to another. Business first, the parameters of territory. Then they begin to play, hardly noticing as, one by one, the other dogs leave the park to go home.

Mingus's master is tall and attractive. Young, I decide, with my usual trace of envy and displacement. In her late twenties, I judge, a place I used to be a couple of decades ago. It will be a few months before I am gratified to learn she's older than this — at a point, to my surprise, when it has begun to matter.

Sometimes I am struck by an embarrassed regret, not about my lost youth, but about the conventional accomplishments I have failed to amass in my appointed time. I suppose I achieved them previously, but now they're gone. It's true that I should be more successful, at least in the conventional sense, than I am at this age; I don't have a home or an acceptable career. But these things no longer hold much attraction for me, because when I *did* have them they didn't provide me with happiness or fulfillment. The trick, for me, is to continue to rise above the embarrassment I'm supposed to feel in not having them. It's not the young people I meet who make me ashamed of myself. They don't care enough to be surprised to encounter someone grey-haired and struggling. No, the inadequacy I feel is something I impose on myself, by contrasting my achievements with conventional expectations of where I am supposed to be at this stage in my life. Somehow, whenever I make this comparison, I invariably discover that I am lacking. It's an old habit I learned in childhood: blaming myself for not living up to standards set by someone else. To live a private life, I must continually resist such critical self-judgment. For those of us trained to adhere to its precepts, conventional life is as addictive as heroin. The withdrawal symptoms one endures on the way to becoming one's own person are so arduous they can drive you mad.

Now that we are alone, the young woman and I introduce ourselves, although with first names only. We exchange the names of our dogs, standing some distance from them, watching them wrestling.

"Well, *they've* certainly hit it off," she says.

"I'd say so," I reply.

We are satisfied to watch them play. They are tireless and we are pleased for them. An hour passes as we exchange their histories, recount their exploits like proud parents, and relate anecdotes we have collected over time.

I learn that Mingus is Alaskan malamute and German shepherd. I hear about the steel plate in his right leg, the result of a car accident when he was younger. I discover that he, like Lupus, was retrieved from the city pound. She calls him Mingus Parker, after the two Charlies from the world of jazz.

I tell her that I have tracked down Lupus's history gradually. I tell her that he came out of the woods northwest of the city when he was just a pup, one parent a wolf, the other some mixture of husky or German shepherd and wolf, and that he spent the first year of his life among humans tied up behind someone's garage until, considered destructive, he was taken to the animal shelter. I even tell her how he helps me satiate my need to be truly myself; he feeds the free-spirited side of my nature, the part of me that, before I knew him, I lacked the courage to acknowledge.

As we talk, our two charges behave like reacquainted siblings renewing an old bond, rather than the strangers they actually are. We're quite impressed, this young woman and I, by how much Mingus and Lupus enjoy each other's company, how easily they've become comrades.

By now I've decided that she is very pretty. She wears a pair of large silver earrings I particularly like. And, for a change, she hasn't asked me why I named my dog after a disease, as so many people do. I don't have to explain that Lupus's name refers to the part of him that is wolf. She's already aware of the Latin *Canis lupus.*

For a long time we fidget in the cold and the snow as the dogs continue to play. I must take Lupus home soon, but he is having so much fun that I decide to stay a little longer, knowing the activity is good for him. Eventually, though, the dogs grow tired. We begin our ceremony of departure, affixing leashes, petting the dogs, settling them down. We say how nice it was to meet one another, then we go our separate ways.

This meeting doesn't feel like destiny in any way, but I'll try to remember it that way later, the way we always do when we meet someone we ultimately love.

I drive downtown for coffee before Lupus and I head home, and I head to a café I frequent. Sometimes I write at a table in a corner not far from the salad bar. I park in one of the city's parking garages and leave Lupus in the car. He has a blanket and cushions in the back to keep him comfortable. He is used to my habits; he'll take a nap while I'm gone.

The café is nothing special, although it would like to be. It has been evolving gradually into a restaurant and I know that, sometime in the future, I'll end up feeling more comfortable somewhere else. There's no middle ground these days. To be prosperous, people must eventually cater exclusively to the prosperous. Or they must exploit the losses of the poor, stocking their pawn shops or secondhand stores with what the poor have been forced to give up.

I order black coffee and a bagel. I won't write here today. I've lingered too long with Mingus and his master. Lunchtime is approaching and soon I'll give up my table to customers with more money to spend.

I was not raised in an environment where people were writers. I was raised in an environment where people got a job. Something secure, safe, acceptable in its conformity. Even when

I began to publish my short stories so many years ago, writing wasn't a respectable enough vocation to be legitimate. It wasn't safe. And risk, to society, is something that is strangely embarrassing. Safety is like wearing clothes, and risk is like walking around in the nude. Except in the world of business perhaps, where one can risk one's money and never risk oneself.

To me, writing is an act that resembles Lupus dashing headlong through the woods. When Lupus sprints through the woods, he runs under fallen tree trunks with but an inch of clearance, certain he can make it without injury. He knows his capabilities, and he knows that the headlong dash, the joy in his momentum, is worth the chance of harm.

Sometimes, when I see him tearing through a densely cluttered wood, I imagine running alongside him, exhilarated. And life, for me, becomes a matter of loving the quiet experience, the celebration in each breath. When I take on too much obligation or look ahead too much, my feet grow heavy as lead and I come to a painful halt, afraid to continue on. But I believe I can find the tenuous, narrow balance between the two extremes because Lupus is showing me the way.

Lupus and I drive the fifty miles or so to spend Christmas with my parents. I take inexpensive gifts: books, wool scarves, gloves. Because I am spending three days with them, I also take my guitar.

I am not a good musician. Sometimes I compose songs for my own amusement or to create something in a matter of days (instead of the many months or years normally demanded by a book), seeing it through quickly from beginning to end. My brother, who lives out west, made his living with the guitar until he was nearly thirty. He launched his career in rock, becoming proficient in folk, jazz, and even classical. He toured most areas of Canada with a number of bands, playing clubs and bars, ultimately switching to country that blended with rock. A single parent, he gave up touring so that his son could live a more conventional life.

While not professionals like my brother was, my parents play the piano and sing for pleasure. They have sung in various community and church choirs and chorales. My mother was a Sweet Adeline, my father sang in a barbershop quartet. While I was growing up, someone was always performing music; in my house, music was the art everyone understood. Writing stories didn't make the same sense to them that making music did. Inadvertently I was pushed to the outside of the family unit, until I lurked on its fringes in disappointment and anger, misunderstood and troublesome, a sheep compelled by circumstance to turn gradually black.

Nothing changes much. I ring their doorbell and it plays "Deck the Halls." I hear the melody filling the house before my father opens the door. He's recently retired and retirement looks good on him here at the door: he's wearing slippers and sports a carefully trimmed moustache. Stocky, he is shorter than I am by three or four inches.

"I hope you're going to play that thing with the door closed," is the first thing he says, glancing at my guitar. He isn't joking.

"Of course," I tell him quickly, although I feel like turning around and taking Lupus back home.

My mother makes coffee. She has had a heart condition for

about fifteen years and this has aged her a bit. I get my height from my mother. She seems to be doing well.

When I visit my parents these days, I feel like I am being interviewed by the acquiescent society I dropped out of a few years ago.

"Have you found a job yet?" they want to know.

"Nothing beyond the contract work I'm doing," I explain. "And there's the Anne Murray book. I'm getting by okay, as far as I'm concerned."

My parents don't ask about the Anne Murray book much. Perhaps when the book actually comes out, they'll be more interested in it.

My mother asks me if I am going to get a haircut. "I liked it better when it wasn't so long," she says.

"It can't help to have long hair when you're looking for a full-time job," my father chimes in.

I reply, "I clean up well when I have to."

Lupus provides a distraction within the antagonism between my parents and me as my parents' dog, Pepper, a Pomeranian, growls at him because Lupus is intruding on his territory. Lupus only dozes, ignoring him, believing he belongs. "Oh, Pepper," my mother says finding this a humorous moment in which to stop interrogating me, "quit your growling. If he wanted to, Lupus could eat you for lunch." Still, Lupus is always welcome to visit my parents because, unlike his human master, he's so well behaved.

Where their older son is concerned, my parents worry often about how things *look*. My mother is candid about this. "I find it hard to mention you to our friends, to your relatives," she says. "They think you're some kind of beatnik or something."

"It isn't importantant what they think," I say.

"That's your trouble," my father says. "You never learned to tow the line."

I sigh, feeling trapped here in their living room, the lights on the Chistmas tree a few feet away from me twinkling incessantly. I suppose what my father says is true, although I am rather proud of it. My personal authenticity compels me to resist blind adherence to a status quo I do not respect. "I'm not going to argue with you, Dad. You like the status quo. I'm not so enamoured of it. Why can't we just agree to disagree?"

But this seems impossible to me. My parents want me to be what they want me to be. They want me to be somebody else.

We take a break for lunch. Afterwards my sons, home for Christmas from college, will drop in for the rest of the day. Their mother and I have been divorced for many years and we are used to arranging Christmas and Boxing Day to accommodate seeing our progeny during the holidays. The divorce is an additional bone of contention between my parents and me. When we first separated so long ago, my father wrote me a letter, threatening to disinherit me. I told him whatever he did was his decision. In the end, the threat didn't come to much; I didn't hear about it again.

When my sons arrive, I greet them at the door as my father greeted me. But there are hugs this time. I must reach up to them for our embrace because they are tall. My older son is dark and tends to resemble his mother. His brother, nearly two years younger, taller than both of us, is fair-haired and is said to resemble me. Whenever I see them, I am mystified by how grown up they continue to be. I am proud of them. They are handsome and intelligent. I enjoy their company whenever we can arrange it. Lupus doesn't see them enough to form much of a bond, because they are some distance away at different schools, but he acknowledges their arrival in his typically aloof way, standing stiffly at the top of the stairs a few feet from the home's entrance, watching our greetings with detached interest.

As we gather in the living room to talk before opening gifts, my father shows off in front of my sons. Some of his antagonism with me takes another form. He manages in a short span of time to bait me politically.

"It's the unions," he says at one point. "All this trouble we're in is the fault of the unions. People aren't satisfied with what they have."

"You were in a union, Dad. Look at what it did for you, your pension, medical benefits."

'It's just greed," my father says. "People being too big for their britches, that's what's wrong with the world."

Later he picks on Quebec and the French. After that, he complains about people on welfare swilling beer and living the high life, knowing these views annoy me and will lead to argument. I ran for the NDP in the 1988 federal election and lost. I have dedicated many hours of my life to a point of view that is opposite that of my father's. We cannot convert each other. I wish we would stop trying.

Pepper growls at Lupus some more. Lupus studiously ignores him.

We are saved from further argument by the Christmas rituals

of opening gifts and working together to prepare Christmas dinner.

"Gee, Dad," my older son says to me at some point when we are out of earshot, grinning and shaking his head. "It's kind of amazing you aren't a bigot."

I chuckle. "I guess it is," I say.

Two months go by before Lupus and I encounter Mingus and his pretty, young companion again.

She remarks in an ambivalent way that it's been quite some time since we first met.

We're in Victoria Park again, at the same time of day, but now it's February, my traditionally hopeless month.

Not much has changed for me. I still owe my landlady rent and I still wait for small cheques that never seem to arrive. But I sleep well each night, I write each day, and every week Lupus and I hike with friends in Frontenac Park, a provincial wilderness park several miles north of here. Our life is uncomplicated, sometimes too much so. Freedom and boredom are never far removed from one another. It all depends on how you choose to look at it.

Lupus and Mingus are glad to see one another after so long. But it's nearly noon and the young woman cannot stay, she has to work in a few hours. When we part this time, we are strangely reserved, as if the long gap between this meeting and our first has soured whatever connection we had made.

March comes. Winter hangs on, malicious winds burst nastily around each corner, driving bands of bitter sleet. By chance

I run into Mingus's master in my café, then again in a downtown restaurant. The four of us meet up a number of times in the park. I discover with wry amusement that I start to look for her the way Lupus looks for Mingus whenever we come to the park, wondering why they do not appear on those days we need them to.

Soon, however, we begin to arrange these periods of play for Lupus and Mingus.

"I'm in town Tuesday," I say casually. "I could bring Lupus here around ten."

Then, around the middle of the month, I decide to ask her out for coffee. But before I can, she invites *me* to coffee at her home not far away.

We fall into a new pattern: meeting in the park to permit Lupus and Mingus to play, returning to her home for coffee. While the dogs nap in the wake of their play, we sit on her living room sofa and talk about books, life, and our respective checkered pasts. It turns out that she writes, as well, although not professionally. We talk about writing—what it does, what it doesn't do, what it accomplishes, what it can never accomplish. We run the gauntlet of obstacles and barbs inherent to the craft.

She is ten years older than I judged her to be. I am careful to conceal from her how relieved I am by this. I am careful to conceal from myself that I am relieved at all.

I tell her about three past marriages that withered on the vine of too much obligation, that collapsed because only half of me was truly married. The other half remained disconnected, gasping in the background of the relationship. For her part, my new friend blames her own bad judgment for her past relationships. She feels the need to be more cautious, to look more carefully beneath the surface of men she becomes interested in.

Soon we are comfortable friends.

On these days in her home, I find myself warning her about all of the things I believe are wrong with me. For instance, I explain to her why, at this relatively late stage in life, I have no money. I am adamant that I have dropped out of a mean-spirited Darwinian society, surprised and a little regretful that I didn't do so earlier. I have political reasons, I explain. I have dropped out because the cyclical pattern of human existence never seems to improve for very long. We are still fighting the same battles, I say, and trying to resolve the same issues that inspired the French Revolution. I'm tired of this, of *it;* I want to live my own life. I've done my bit, I explain, writing articles, elected to a municipal council a decade ago in Gananoque, running in the federal election. I've been a party to the endless conflict, now I want to be much less involved. Or more. I haven't decided yet.

She listens and smiles, forewarned. I am a lousy choice for a partner. I just want her to know.

Each day, as we talk and drink coffee, as Lupus and Mingus doze not far away on the floor, they demonstrate so much patience for this slow dance of acquaintanceship. And gradually I move into that anxious no man's land that divides friendship and romance.

I grow strangely complacent about falling in love with her. There is no desperation involved, no longing in the way I care for her. I consider it just something extra to enjoy about my life. This is the first time I've begun to fall in love without compromising myself, without feeling a terrifying desperation over whether I am socially acceptable or not.

The month of March passes this way, then she and Mingus visit our home in Yarker to see where Lupus and I live. It is still cold. Spring remains moody and sour. Today grey clouds mass over slim cracks of promising blue sky. What remains of winter does not want to give in.

By now I know Mingus hates cats. I have seen him give ferocious chase on six or seven occasions, whenever a cat has strolled into his field of vision. Afterwards, Mingus must be restrained until he settles down. When we arrive at my home, Mingus and his master must wait outside on the deck while I reinforce the accordion screen separating my quarters from the rest of the house to make sure my landlady's cat doesn't come to harm. Mingus's master has said that the two dining room chairs will not be enough. I add a couple of heavy boxes from the closet in this room.

Mingus knows the house contains something we don't want him to notice. No sooner has he entered my apartment than he positions himself at the barricaded door, tilting his head this way and that, as though he can detect the cat on the other side. Charlie is there, looking for trouble, perhaps contemplating the Pandora's box my quarters have become. When I peer through the crack in my folding doors, I can see him sitting on the other side, reinforcing the old saw about curiosity and the cat.

Lupus is no help. He merely curls up at the side of my bed, like all of this is my fault and I deserve the anxiety I feel about Mingus's preoccupation with Charlie. Mingus is a big dog, and even my reinforced barricade doesn't appear strong enough to hold him back for long. It's not a case of if but *when* he'll charge through my doors to chase the cat flirting dangerously on the other side.

His master has brought lunch, and I've promised her dinner. Lupus is not a mooch, but Mingus is. As we eat biscuits stuffed with tuna or cheese, he's distracted enough by the food to forget about the cat. Lupus ignores lunch, remaining by the side of my bed.

When lunch is over, my friend and I talk. Neither of us is short of things to say. While we talk, Mingus returns to his vigil at the barricade, listening for the cat at large somewhere in the house.

"I think we should take these guys for a walk," his master says.

The afternoon has warmed up a little. Pale sunlight leaks through the cloud cover with a sickly half-heartedness. Wearing gloves, hats, and nylon parkas, our animals connected to us by leashes, we amble in the direction of a snowmobile trail at the northern edge of the village. Lupus and I walked this trail a couple of times last autumn because it was quiet and there were wooded areas where we could commune with the fall colours. Today, however, melting snow, spring runoff, and thick mud have transformed sections of it into a bog.

"Whaddyuh think?" I ask my companion as we stand on the verge of the first muddy obstacle.

"Ah, what the hell," she says with a cheerful shrug.

We continue on, Lupus and Mingus straining at their leashes, excited to be outside, wading through puddles and dancing over ruts of mud while their masters leap from one grassy tuft to another, trying to keep dry and laughing at their circumstances.

"I hope these animals know what we go through for them," my companion says.

Our high spirits — the result of an optimistic spring fever in all our souls — bring inspiration to this walk, but eventually my companion and I take a break before we must head back. We sit on the top rail of a dilapidated cedar rail fence at the edge of the path. Brown grasses rise to reclaim the fence, and we rest our boots on the ground. We look out over a rolling panorama of farmland, a distant farmhouse and partially collapsed barn. There are valleys of melting snow and gentle hillocks blown bare, with sere, lifeless grasses on their crowns. Ponds of run-off stir in the wind, their waters a grey chop.

Lupus curls up near my feet, used to the periodic breaks we take when we hike. Mingus, barely two years old, is restless, already anxious to get going again. He paces back and forth, impatient with the two humans sitting on the fence nearby, chatting happily with one another.

My companion and I sit close, nearly close enough to touch. I contemplate taking her hand but I do not.

"Do you have extra towels?" my companion asks in the midst of my reverie.

"Sorry?"

"Extra towels for the dogs? I didn't think to bring any with me."

"Oh, sure," I reply. Despite my humble means, I *do* have lots of towels.

We return to the house. When we arrive, I scrounge a wash basin and fill it with lukewarm water. Then we wash our dogs and towel them down, while they gently object to these necessary ablutions.

As we accomplish these labours, I tell her about Lupus's encounter with a skunk at the bottom of the yard last October. I let him out to do his business just before bedtime and, noticing the skunk, he dashed off to give chase. "Lupus?" I cried in alarm when I recognized what he was after. I can't say for sure whether it was instinct or a change of heart, but at the last instant — even as the skunk sprayed in self-defence — he leaped over it and hurried back to me, virtually unscathed.

"There was a little yellow patch on his neck, smaller than my thumbnail," I explain. "It was like he realized he was making a mistake, that it was a skunk and he'd best leave it alone."

"I wish Mingus had realized he was making a mistake," my companion says, and proceeds to tell me about a much more disastrous encounter with a skunk in her backyard last summer. Mingus was sprayed full in the face. The stench was so powerful it wafted inside the house from the yard.

"Mingus wasn't the only one green around the gills. It nearly made *me* sick as well."

Inside, we drink Valpolicella while I prepare a curried chicken dish at the stove in my landlady's kitchen. My landlady arrived home from work earlier, prepared a vegetarian meal for herself and then departed, leaving the kitchen to us. Mingus remains with Lupus on the other side of the barricade. They fuss periodically at their imprisonment.

Inspired by the wine, Mingus's master and I flirt. On the one hand, our conversation is the same as it always is. On the other, it has a new edge. We laugh frequently or gaze at each other for an extra second or two before we turn away, still smiling.

I enjoy the pleasant tension. I feel alive, though aware that some of my blurred intensity should be attributed to drinking, something I can afford to do only rarely. As I cook, my companion grows even more beautiful, sitting at the table. She has large blue eyes and her earrings dance against her cheeks. I drift through the meal preparations, browning this, slicing that, stirring the resulting concoction in a haze. This hour or so passes in a warm glow. I appreciate its quiet hopefulness, the way it gently vibrates.

Before we sit down to eat, we must feed the dogs. Mingus is such a glutton, my companion says, he's sure to covet Lupus's food as well. Better they be kept apart. So we give Lupus his meal in the kitchen, while Mingus must remain in my apartment on the other side of the barricade.

After dinner, we rejoin Mingus on the other side of the barricade, where we take coffee. I have made a full pot. When my companion wishes to go home, I want to have eliminated what remains of the wine's effects so that I can drive.

"So what's the agenda?" she asks me as we drink our coffee.

I didn't expect this question. Guiltily, all I can think about is assuring her that she is safe with me. She is my friend and I have not brought her here to confine her so that I can make advances.

"Agenda?" I stammer.

"Yes."

"Well I've made lots of coffee. I'll be able to drive you and Mingus home. Just let me know when you're ready to leave."

She nods, her face a mask.

"I should take Mingus out for a pee," she says.

"Okay."

While she is outside, I contemplate this new awkwardness between us. I feel I must explain something to her, but I'm not clear on how to do it. How can I explain that I appreciate her friendship but that—yes, as well—I am deeply attracted to her? How do I describe the innocence in something like that, when in all probability it will not be perceived innocently? I fear losing her friendship. I do not want her to feel uncomfortable with me, or at risk in any way, now or in the future.

When she returns with Mingus I pour us more coffee while she unleashes him. We are silent. I feel something is going wrong, maybe everything.

"Sometimes," I say, mustering my courage, "when a man is friends with a woman, he doesn't want to admit he's attracted to her for fear of losing her friendship. You know?"

She nods.

I go on. It becomes a surprisingly long speech that meanders, abstractedly coursing through the landscape of my dilemma, passing by markers of my respect for a woman's safety and my comprehension of the quandary that results when romance abuts onto an established friendship. I explore what can potentially be lost if both people don't feel the same way, how awkward the friendship can become. No wonder this speech is so long. As I squirm, I finally acknowledge to myself that I am falling in love with her. I don't mention this to her, of course.

She listens to all I say, smiling gently at my awkwardness.

"So," I conclude finally. "I wouldn't do anything to spoil our friendship. I just wanted you to know that."

"Okay," she says.

"I didn't bring you here to—you know."

"I know that."

More things are said to walk us around our discomfort.

"When I went outside with Mingus earlier," she tells me, "it was because I was upset. I thought you just wanted to be friends."

"No," I say. "I don't just want to be friends."

In the end, she decides to stay. Somehow we manage an embrace, a kiss, ultimately to make love.

"I think you truly are who you say you are," she tells me afterwards.

We have been chortling about my speech, how long and clumsy it was.

"But you meant it, didn't you?"

"I did. I was petrified I was going to frighten you off."

I feel a tremendous peace come over me, as though all four of us have found our places in some humble new circumstance. Lupus sleeps by my bed. Mingus stakes out a spot on the carpet in the other room. We feel like family — an unconventional family of people, dog, and wolf-dog, perhaps, but family just the same. This moment, this night, all of it, becomes inviolate, as if now that this long moment has achieved a near-perfection it swears an oath to never change. Although something deep inside me knows my conclusion is foolish (change always lurks just beyond the hour or two we wish would stand still) I do not worry on this night about what, if anything, can be taken from me. Instead I bask in the possibilities of whatever lies ahead.

I am compelled to remain awake after my girlfriend falls asleep. It's both excitement and the calm of *being,* I decide. I feel this calm deeply and clearly.

Without consciously deciding to do so, I reach down and touch Lupus at the side of my bed, sharing my pleasure with him, wanting him to know that I am at peace, wanting to acknowledge his role in what has taken place. He makes no sound, doesn't move. But I find him still there in the morning when I happily wake up, tangible evidence, perhaps, that what has changed for me has changed at last for good.

September 1995

We sit in a small clearing, the woods behind us drawn across the gentle valley like a curtain, a broad, algae-scummed swamp cut into the lowlands languishing just in front. It's early autumn, the kind of fall day that refuses to relinquish summer's glamour. Birds call, twitter, and sing. Insects hum: dragonflies and bluebottles, anachronistic mosquitoes. The air is thick with sunlight. It buzzes and shimmers egotistically. Blue sky, with white clouds passing slowly overhead, and below trees, both deciduous and coniferous, a dusty, dark, complacent green. Brown, red, and gold are only moments away, as soon as cooler temperatures arrive to impose their ritual change on the landscape. But for now this departing summer has been such a splendid season it's grown full of itself.

Lupus and I have been hiking one of the shorter trails in Frontenac Park. Usually we navigate this network of trails with friends, but today we are alone. I have brought a notebook because I want to write in the sanctuary of the wilderness, which is where I'm now convinced I probably belong. We have stopped to eat lunch in this clearing, then I intend to write for an hour or so. Lupus is content with the longer break. He does not eat when we hike; he doesn't like carrying food in his belly while we pick our way along the park's rugged trails. In our early days together I'd bring dog biscuits in my pockets, but I don't bother any longer. He only buried them and, over time, I recognized the futility of feeding the wilderness in this way. Lupus caches food whenever he can, like he's planning ahead for the day I cannot afford to feed him. I eat a sandwich, an apple, and a small wedge of cheese. I offer Lupus some cheese, one of his favourite treats, but, as usual, because we are hiking, he declines it by turning his head away.

Food, for Lupus, is purely functional. He's never impatient for it, never gorges on it, and rarely begs for anything. About once a month, as if he's aware he's gained some weight, he goes on a two- or three-day fast, ignoring any food I serve him. At first I fretted that he was ill when he refused to eat, but gradually I learned his fasts keep him trim, purge his deft body of any impurities he believes might slow him down. And the part of him that is wolf, I've discovered, is more nutritionally efficient than the part of him that is dog, and is better able to store and ration the nutrients derived from his food. I've been told that if he were a full-blown wolf he'd only need to eat once a week.

Still, he seems to enjoy our current hiatus. He rests but doesn't sleep. He lies down and studies his surroundings, his ears cocked, his nostrils flaring as he absorbs and filters scents floating on the breeze. I speculate that he grows philosophical, that he feels the same belonging I feel in this wooded wilderness. Lupus enjoys these long moments of silent reflection even more if we've climbed to higher ground. He likes to scale the highest available rock and lie on its summit, gazing out over the panorama his vantage point presents. When he does this, he reminds me of a monarch administering his kingdom, gazing down on it in responsible benevolence.

Although I can detect a hint of the bounty such occasions provide for him, that is the limit of what I can achieve. As a human, it may be that I can only glimpse this kind of tranquility or self-assurance. Unlike Lupus, I must strain moments such as these through a sieve of social pressures and doubts about my function, my usefulness, and the money I must earn to live and to legitimate my place in society. Humans, I believe, are unique in the demands placed upon them; they are the only species on Earth compelled to justify to their peers their right to be alive. They must sow, harvest, and stockpile achievements, possessions, or excuses to assert that their existence has value. If they are unable — or unwilling — to amass points in this way, they must apologize to their tribe for what they have failed to become. When Lupus lies in regal splendour atop one summit or another, gazing at the earth unfurling below him, he reveals himself to be in contrast to human society, which has evolved in a more narrow, rigid fashion.

Lupus and I are not on high ground today. Nonetheless there's a partial vista we can enjoy. The swamp in the foreground is toothpicked in places by dead, limbless trees reaching grey and naked towards the skies. One of these is crowned by a twisted network of twigs I recognize as an abandoned blue heron's nest. Beyond this, in the distance, an abstract quilt of rocks, trees, and meadow gradually rises towards a deeper woods.

I lean against a tree, writing in a scribbler I pin against my knees. Between sentences or paragraphs, I glance at my companion lying a few yards from me and wonder what he is thinking. Sometimes I marvel at his fierce independence, that helps me love him so much, that connects us so perfectly.

When I finish writing, I cap my pen, close my scribbler, and return both to the knapsack that leans against my leg. I glance at Lupus again, then detect movement beyond him in the trees. Unannounced, a stag strolls into the opening about twenty-five yards from where Lupus lies, its head erect, its entire bearing large and proud.

Lupus is up and moving before I can reach out and grab the collar around his neck. The stag darts towards the swamp—its hooves pounding, the sound reverberating like an earthquake through the ground on which I sit—Lupus in pursuit. I call to him to come back because I fear for him. The stag is big, mature, and experienced; I don't want Lupus to be hurt.

I soon fall silent, as I realize what is going to take place. I watch in admiration as the deer's strategy unfolds. It leaps gracefully over and around the obstacles in the swamp, its white tail erect, and gains the other side in a matter of seconds. Lupus, however, bogs down in the mud and muck of the swamp before he is even halfway across, his usual speed completely compromised by the stag's experienced tactics.

I can't help laughing at his dilemma. I have no idea if he is embarrassed by this turn of events, but I like to think he is because he's so cocky most of the time. He turns at the sound of my mirth. Then, refusing to give in, he turns back again, still seeking the stag. But the deer has already vanished, absorbed into the trees on the other side of the swamp.

"C'mon, Loop," I call. "He's gone."

After a moment's hesitation, Lupus returns. He's a terrible mess, mud caked on or dripping from his white legs and belly. He smells of muck and decaying vegetation, the thick stew the swamp has become this time of year. I stroke him behind the ears before I refasten his leash. On the way back we will pass along the shore of one of the park's more tranquil lakes. There I'll clean the mud from him.

"He's too experienced for a guy like you," I say, as Lupus turns for a final wistful glance across the swamp.

He's accepted that the stag was too much for him. He's forgiven the stag for besting him.

I've noticed such casual acceptance before about incidents in the wilderness: humiliations or disappointments are always brief, quickly forgotten, even irrelevant. They're not collected, gathered, or stored in vast bins, to be linked into long chains of endless failure dragged from place to place the way they are in human society. There's no comparison exercised here, no cataloguing of shortcomings, no condemning those shortcomings as sins. Out here in the woods, there's an instinctive state of honour — not a code — that we humans have forgotten in our zeal to build a society defined by what we feel we must amass.

As long as Lupus has been with me, he has wanted to run with the deer. This is one of the reasons I keep him leashed most of the time. I have come to know Frontenac Park quite intimately. There are places where I can expect to encounter deer, other areas where both Lupus and I can enjoy a brief respite from the tedium of being confined by his leash. Even so, unleashing Lupus at all has its risks, although most of the time it works out happily enough.

Also, a park rule states that all dogs must be leashed at all times. The park warden explained to me one morning, when I first began to bring Lupus here, that many people believe this rule exists to protect the wildlife, but actually the reverse is true. "It's the dogs that'll get injured, not the wildlife," he said, wanting to be sure I knew the rules about leashes.

In Lupus's case, this assumption is only partially true. He's less vulnerable to injury in the wilderness than most dogs. Granted, I've pulled porcupine quills from his nose on two occasions: once during winter when he stuck his snout into a snowdrift at the end of a fallen log, then again one spring afternoon when he encountered a porcupine out in the open. That second time he was ahead of me on the trail and I didn't witness the skirmish. And, being Lupus, he was silent, there were no barks or yelps. He came to me both times to show me what was wrong. Fortunately on both occasions I was with friends, and together we were able to pull the quills out quickly (five the first time, ten the second). Lupus suffered this painful exercise with surprising patience, whining briefly as each quill was torn out, the barbs catching in his tender flesh. He knew what had to be done and cooperated until each quill was removed. He resisted my ministrations only once, and then only slightly, when I had to remove one last quill embedded in the flesh of the underside of his tongue.

Then, last autumn, he darted down a hill after three full-grown raccoons he spotted in a stand of trees at the edge of a pond. I saw him disappear over the crest of the hill and, as I gave chase, I heard the sounds of an altercation from below. I heard Lupus bellow; I later discovered that one of the raccoons had already taken refuge in a nearby tree. The third was doing a three-sixty in the air well above Lupus's head, where, in annoyance, he had tossed it. I called out for him to come, and he responded, paying heed to the frantic quality in my voice. The third raccoon seized the opportunity to join its companions in the tree.

But deer have always enticed Lupus most. When we see them on the trail, usually in the distance, he tugs at his leash until they disappear from view. It's not that he wants to hurt them or bring one of them down. Rather they present him with a game, a spirited sprint through the woods. During the first spring of our relationship, Lupus emerged from the woods some distance from the house we rented then, gambolling in the twilight behind a group of eight deer. He kept his distance, jogging and leaping a few yards behind them until I called him off. When he turned to obey, the deer slipped back into the woods, unharmed.

This past spring, though, an incident near the end of March troubled me for a time. Spring had arrived relatively early, and the ice on the park's lakes was thin. I'd unleashed Lupus because this was not an area usually frequented by deer, and he had vanished into the trees just ahead of us. I was walking with two friends in single file along a narrow trail skirting a lake.

Suddenly one of my friends shouted a warning, and both of them leaped off the trail. A young deer was dashing directly towards me, Lupus trotting along behind it in characteristically gleeful silence. I hurried out of the way, afraid the charging deer would knock me down.

"Lupus!" I cried sternly, after the deer passed.

He continued on for a couple of yards, then he stopped and turned back. As usual, his leash was coiled around my neck. I reached for it as, panting with enthusiasm, he came to stand beside me. However, in the distance the inexperienced deer had begun to complicate matters. In a panic it had taken to the thin ice covering the lake. Now, about twenty-five yards from shore, it found itself in difficulty. Lupus bolted after it again before I could connect him to his leash, some predatory instinct kicking in as he realized the deer was trapped on the thin ice and now probably at his mercy. Indeed, the animal was in grave circumstances. One rear leg had broken through the ice. As it pulled this one out, the other broke through. This pattern repeated itself a couple of times as the deer tried to extricate itself. Lupus, on the other hand, was unimpeded by the treacherous surface of the lake. Spreading his paws on the ice, a talent of his I'd seen before, he was able to advance quickly on the hapless deer.

By that point I was running at full speed towards the lake, Lupus's leash dangling in my hands, my knapsack thumping against my back. I was an alarmed collage of reactions: fear, frustration, compassion, disgust. All of these could be heard in my shrieking voice as I tried to call off my wolf-dog. Lupus, manifesting some disturbing amalgam of excitement and calm, kept circling the terrified deer, looking for the best vantage point from which to press his attack. As I reached the shore, the ice too thin for me to proceed any further, I saw him tear a large chunk of flesh out of the deer's hindquarters.

"Lupus," I screamed. "Come here! Right now!"

He hesitated a moment.

"Lupus!"

Astonishingly — even miraculously — he finally obeyed.

As he reached the shore, I could see that his face was smeared with blood. I grabbed his collar and quickly leashed him. We turned away from the lake, me with some insistence, Lupus a dead weight of regret on his end of the leash. Slowly we stumbled back up the trail. Finally, when I decided we were a safe distance away, I stopped and glanced back at the deer in time to see it awkwardly leave the ice. Once it gained the shore, it darted safely into the woods.

My friends and I washed the blood from Lupus's face in a section of lake further along the shore, where the ice had already melted. I bemoaned aloud the injury to the deer, feeling responsible for the tragedy that had nearly taken place. But my friends concluded the damage had been slight.

"It's instinct," one of them said. "He can't help it. Part of him is programmed to hunt."

I acknowledged this view, although guiltily. "I suppose so."

I thought about an incident that had occurred about four months earlier. As my friends and I stood among the boulders strewn along a trail that forks off to the north, at the edge of a narrow lake, some wolves began to howl from a hidden location among the rocks and trees on the other side of the water. We froze, unafraid but mesmerized. We couldn't see them — in fact, *never* saw them — but their howling was so close and eerie there could be no doubt that they were relatively nearby. At their cries, Lupus moved ten yards closer to the lake and sat down for several moments, clearly listening to what they said. I felt they were calling out to him. Alarmed, I stole up behind him and leashed him. I feared they might entice him away from me. I feared, should he be tempted to go to them, they would tear him to pieces, concluding that he was some neutered, hybrid intruder that didn't belong among them. Not long afterwards, the howling abruptly ceased. Soon Lupus was happy to continue our hike, the crying wolves forgotten.

Lupus, his face cleaned of the deer's blood, sat by my leg and gazed up at me, no doubt mystified by my mood. After a moment I patted him on the head because he'd come when I called him.

I recognized then the two sides of his nature, *his* duality: the canine guilt he displayed over misbehaving and the wolfishness that had compelled him to try to bring down the deer because, for thousands of years, it has been his prey. For a long time afterwards, I sympathized with him, recognizing aspects of his duality that were so much like my own. I puzzled over questions of instinct versus reason, and how we find some balance between them. Is one more right than the other? What makes this question so difficult to answer?

Since the incident with the deer on the ice, Lupus has been off his leash rarely as we've explored this park. Only when we are resting in locations I believe safe do I remove his leash. And the fact that this adjustment is not to keep *him* safe, but to keep the wildlife safe — well, that remains our closely guarded secret. I visit Frontenac Park with Lupus throughout the year, except during the height of summer when the insects and the heat conspire to keep us away. Mostly, out of deference to the working schedule of my friends, we wait until the weekends, usually Sundays, so that we'll have company on our hikes. It's rare that Lupus and I come here alone.

The park is a significant distance from where we live, and I try to ration my gas. Lupus and I ration everything. We save up to pay our rent, stockpile food when a cheque comes in, buy gasoline for the car in five- or ten-dollar increments. I do make *some* money, hiring out my writing services or related experience in promotion or marketing, preparing and delivering newsletters and other documents for a municipal government in the Kingston area or creating news releases and other documents about books and authors for a local publisher. But the income is so uncertain and sporadic, I must be careful how and when I spend. And sometimes the cheques are late. Even though most of the people I deal with are familiar with my circumstances, they too often must be hounded for payment. I have despised this fact for a long time, and I still don't understand it. "It's just business," they usually say, as if this explains everything.

I come to the park with Lupus to refresh myself. It is one of three distinct worlds I have come to know with varying degrees of intimacy in recent months. This one, relatively untamed, apparently more fundamental, accepts me in my strangeness, does not resist my intrusion. It doesn't harangue me about my failings or remind me about what I've lost.

At home, in the small village where Lupus and I rent our quarters, I find a middle ground. It's rural enough that I believe I can keep one foot in the wilderness, and far enough away from the ideologically accelerating torments of urban society that I remain calm and composed. Here, I work and write, edging tentatively towards a future I feel is more of my own making. Here, the peace in my freedom remains. Here, I don't worry much. Here, I retire at night and shortly fall asleep. If I dream, I don't remember it, and I never toss and turn. I wake up refreshed. I don't tangle much with the various social hypocrisies I am unable to reconcile. And here, almost like in the wilderness, society's snide little taunts and comparisons — its focus on greed and power, its notions of flattery and insult — do not reach out for me in any persistent or meaningful way.

To live, however, to feed myself and Lupus, to keep a roof over our heads and put gasoline in the car, I must find people who will pay for my services. To meet my meagre obligations, I must do business in Kingston. If the wilderness sometimes seems like heaven, and my small home resembles purgatory, then the city is probably hell: the place where anger, frustration, and doubt must be grappled with.

This antipathy does not exist just because I prefer the rural to the urban, or the natural to the manufactured. My dislike of the city is not as simple as that. No, I feel all of society's ideologies and vapid mythologies collect here in a more intense concentration. When Lupus and I come to the city, we drive by dozens of edifices: churches, legal offices, fire stations, stores, malls, and government buildings. Signs and parking meters, arrows and oasis parks. We drive by rusty cars and Porsches waxed to a sheen. I think of all of this machinery, all these symbols of conformity, as a wilderness of its own. Yet, unlike the park an hour or so away, there's too much judgment here. The city is the opposite of the wilderness: in the city, too many people must be small to make a few of the others feel big.

In the city, I eat lunch with an old friend I see every few months. He enjoys a good income and won't let me buy. I used to feel bad when he insisted on paying, protesting vehemently, wanting to take my turn, but now I realize he enjoys this kind of generosity. It underscores for him, I think, the gulf that exists between our two worlds and the way our friendship acts as a bridge across that gulf. In a way, I suppose, we both behave like dilettantes, dabbling with each other's sense of place, each of us knowing we don't really belong in the other's world. Of course, he has the advantage of remembering me from a time when I was a much different person, when I lived in circumstances quite similar to his own.

We've eaten and now we're having coffee and updating each other on our personal news. His life seems busier than mine, more hectic. Sometimes I feel a faint embarrassment because not much changes for me in the weeks between each visit. But the feeling evaporates once I leave the city.

He glances at his watch. Soon he must get back to the office where he works.

"Did you bring Lupus?" he asks.

I nod. "He's in the car in the parking garage. If I'm late he'll start to howl."

"You still can't leave him at home?"

"No, he'd just eat the place."

He grins. He's met Lupus. "I wish I had the guts to drop out the way you have," he says.

He's mentioned this before, and my response is always the same. "I don't have a wife and a young child," I remind him. "And you know as well as I do that it was attrition more than courage. It would have been 'guts' if I'd done it a lot earlier, when I had more to lose. It would have meant much more if I'd done it many years ago, when I wanted to but didn't have the nerve."

Silently he reflects on my point of view.

"I know what you're saying, though," I add. "Years ago, I used to have a Hermann Hesse quotation on my wall. Something like: 'too much responsibility or obligation is just lack of courage to lead a private life.'"

Our server brings more coffee and hot water.

As we wind down, I can see he must go back to work. I recognize the signs. There is that faraway look we get when we have a long list of work to do. I can see him ticking off his obligations in his mind. Dropping out, as I have, still entices him. In the end, he'll still want to believe I did it all on my own, exercising some courageous freedom of choice he would like to authorize for himself. Whether he would be successful in pursuing a path similar to the one I've chosen for myself, however, is not something I can say for sure, nor is it fair of me to speculate. It's always easier to desire someone else's life than to recognize what we have in our own. I know this. I've coveted other people's paths too, wanting them to be mine.

I walk him back to his office along downtown streets that smell of car exhaust and clogged storm drains. We say our goodbyes at the edge of the sidewalk near two ticking parking meters. I watch him go inside, then stand for a few minutes at the edge of this busy street to see if I still feel the insistent urban terror brought on by all my failures here, my defeat at the hands of relentless competition. I do. But the feeling only lasts a moment. In fact, it's more like an echo than an actual feeling: the echo of the chronic, relentless fear that once nearly snapped me like a twig. I remember that period often and its endless work, my ill health, the long days spent in hospital. But the memory is gentler now. It is less insistent now that I have a clearer idea of who I really am.

Lupus and I sit in the backyard, me on a lawn chair at the edge of the stoop, Lupus lying on the grass not far away. Charlie is outside, too, cavorting at the bottom of the garden just in front of the shed. It's a pleasant fall evening at the end of September. The leaves are changing but not yet falling from the trees, and the setting sun has a sharp angle to it, capturing us as if in the rays of a giant flashlight. I wear sunglasses, but I also wear a jacket because the evening will soon grow cool. Lupus isn't sleeping, but he lies motionless on the grass, looking a little ragged in places now that his winter coat has begun to come in. White tufts of delicate undercoat are giving way to the coarser fur on the outside. Every now and then I pick out one of these tufts with my fingers, collecting them in a pile on the grass underneath my chair. Mostly, though, both of us are still. I don't even need my evening coffee. This is one of those rare moments when I seem to need nothing at all.

Despite the ennui of this sun-dappled evening, I keep gazing ruefully at a young maple about ten yards away that bears our scars. Earlier this summer, called away suddenly to a meeting with my publisher, I had to chain Lupus to this tree until I returned. There was no one to sit with him, it was too hot to make him wait in the car, and leaving him in our lodgings alone has always been out of the question. Somewhat desperately, then, I chained him to the tree. It was shady, and I knew I wouldn't be long. And I left him a deep bowl of water, ice cubes clinking against the metal sides of the container. By the time I returned less than two hours later, he'd nearly felled the tree. Although the trunk he was tied to was eight or ten inches in circumference, he had gnawed more than two-thirds of the way through.

The damage reflected more than his passion to resist confinement. It demonstrated the power in his jaws and the sharpness of his teeth. Although Lupus is part dog, he does not have a dog's teeth. They are larger than a dog's, angled somewhat differently and razor-sharp. In our early days together, he chewed through a seatbelt in the back seat of my car. I don't know why he did this; there seemed to be no reason other than his frustration at being confined. It took him less than sixty seconds, and he tore it clean in half. I couldn't believe my eyes. Later I discovered that he can lock his jaws. I've seen him do it. With all my strength, I can't pry them apart, the way one can with a normal dog.

That is why I don't wrestle with him. I tried in the early days, as I had wrestled with dogs I owned previously but, although Lupus cut back on his enthusiasm the way dogs do when they play with their masters, he was still too physically overpowering for me. Too fast, too strong, his teeth too sharp.

Those few times we played together, I sustained some minor injuries, especially given his propensity for nipping at any part of my anatomy that presented itself. My wrists would bleed from the sharpness of his teeth. On one occasion, when I was wearing only sweat pants, he nipped me accidentally on the end of my penis, which was a profoundly painful reminder of how strong and quick he was, even during play. Sometimes, infrequently, he'll try to wrestle with me now, especially if he feels he's been denied attention for a time. He gets stubborn about it, too. He insists. In the end, I have to dissuade him by clutching his ruff in both fists, gazing into his eyes, and growling ferociously. This always works. For some reason, he is convinced that the bluff behind my assertion that I am the alpha wolf is based on hierarchical fact.

As I gaze at the injured maple, I can't help but feel vaguely guilty about the damage. Lupus's wilder self, the one that won't be confined, is an essential part of him, yet to live in my world he must be tame. I feel much the same conflict within myself. I don't want to be confined by society's strictures and, like Lupus, I can be destructive. Even to myself.

Soon I notice one of the neighbourhood cats approaching across the lawn next door. It is a tortoiseshell cat that my landlady has complained about in the past because it bullies the other cats in the area. This evening, as I watch its stealthy approach, I realize it is stalking Charlie, who reclines at the bottom of the garden, oblivious and lazy, his back towards his assailant. I lean forward in my chair, not liking what appears to be taking place.

Lupus doesn't like it either. I watch as he carefully eases himself into a crouch.

Tortoiseshell is gazing studiously at Charlie as she deftly creeps in his direction. Lupus, meanwhile, cautiously creeps forward as well. I can't help but be apprehensive, surrounded as I am by so much animal concentration, so much palpable tension. Only Charlie remains unaware of what is taking place.

I have good reason to worry. Lupus's motivation to protect Charlie from ambush is noble, but this would be a poor and not very believable defence if Lupus happened to kill the tortoiseshell cat. I'm not sure of the best thing to do. I know if I suddenly stand up to intercede, Lupus will bolt in the direction of his quarry. Yet I don't have time to intervene in slow motion. As I hesitate, Tortoiseshell creeps closer to Charlie, and Lupus creeps closer to Tortoiseshell. It's clear that I must act.

"Charlie," I call, trying to imitate the melody in my landlady's voice. "Oh, Chaaarlie."

But nothing changes — baritone isn't soprano. Charlie continues to sprawl on the lawn by the shed as the other cat slips closer and Lupus, in turn, stalks her. Then, as I try again to get Charlie's attention, Tortoiseshell suddenly glances in Lupus's direction, noticing him for the first time. Aware of the dilemma she has created for itself, Tortoiseshell freezes. So does Lupus, now barely five yards away. Charlie turns, sees the other cat, glances at Lupus, and, finally aware of the drama that has been unfolding behind his back, gets quickly to his feet. His tail begins to swish menacingly back and forth, and he moves forward slowly to challenge Tortoiseshell. As I watch this deadlock develop, I'm reminded of the final gunfight in *The Good, the Bad and the Ugly*. All that's missing is the lush guitar work of Ennio Morricone's soundtrack and the menacing squints of Clint Eastwood, Eli Wallach, and Lee Van Cleef.

I give Tortoiseshell credit for knowing when to withdraw. Assessing the situation and realizing the futility of pressing her attack, she cautiously turns to go back the way she came. I'm reduced to silent supplication: "Don't run," I plead, knowing that, if Tortoiseshell runs, Lupus will chase her, catch her, and do her harm. But Tortoiseshell doesn't run. She contrives an artful attitude of disdain for the proceedings she precipitated. As nonchalantly as she can, the cat departs, ultimately disappearing around the corner of the house next door. Charlie lies down in the grass again. After a moment, Lupus comes back to lie down by my chair.

"Good to have friends in high places, Charlie," I call, as I stroke Lupus behind the ears, more relieved than they are at the way things worked out. Charlie takes his rescue for granted. He stretches, yawns, and sprawls on the grass. Life is good.

Lupus was attacked by two neighbourhood cats in the village park one afternoon this past summer. It was a warm day and the spring rush of the river had declined, replaced by a laconic drift that didn't accelerate until it approached the falls. Lupus's goose and the three ducks that are its constant companions floated on the river's surface like shiftless vagrants.

As we entered the park, I don't think either of us noticed the cats lurking in a small clump of grass not far from the riverbank. Lupus, as was his ritual, trotted over to this small hummock to leave his territorial mark. As he was about to lift his leg, the two cats pounced on him, screeching aggressively, claws flying.

Although he was outnumbered and surprised by the attack, the cats were unable to connect. As Charlie had discovered when he and Lupus first met, it is not an easy task to strike an animal with Lupus's speed. Lupus merely stepped away from the slashing claws, not enough to withdraw from the altercation, but enough to make it clear that the cats had met their match this time. Again the cats moved in, launching themselves at Lupus's face. Again they failed to connect as he feinted to the left, then darted to the right, effectively separating one cat from the other.

Abandoning their attack, both cats fled, one to the right, the other to the left. The one that went left had but five yards to run before it could safely climb a tree. The other, however, had to dash five times this distance to reach the nearest tree. It was too far. Lupus ran the cat down before it was halfway to safety.

"Lupus," I cried.

The cat was in his mouth, caught by the back of the neck between those potentially lethal jaws. It was strangely docile by now, as if resigned to the fact that it had seriously underestimated the abilities of its antagonist.

"Lupus!"

I suppose he believed he'd made his point. At any rate, if he felt any malice for the cat, it contained little resolve. With an exaggerated nonchalance, he released his captive as if there had been no near-death altercation at all. Behind him, his panicky assailant gained the tree and climbed to safety. As if to emphasize that he had acted entirely out of principle, Lupus lifted his leg on the shrub where he'd been attacked and, as thoroughly as he could, washed it down with his territorial golden stream.

I suspect Lupus's friendship with Charlie is behind his apparent tolerance for cats, but I cannot say for sure. Sometimes, on sunny days, when I am working at my table, I'll turn towards the pool of sunlight on the floor by my two sliding glass doors to find both animals lying there asleep in the rays of the sun. They sprawl on their sides, their backs to one another, touching ever so slightly, furry comrades sharing the sunshine.

They've even tried to play together a couple of times, but it hasn't worked out. Charlie, fat and lazy, wants to lie on his back and bat playfully at Lupus's nose. Lupus, on the other hand, wants Charlie to chase him around the yard. They mystify one another this way. What one considers sport, the other finds incomprehensible. Their attempts to play together, half-hearted and without a common language, never amount to anything. Lupus is one kind of animal. Charlie is another.

Lupus can get jealous of Charlie's intrusions, but even when he does, he expresses his annoyance patiently, as if only to remind Charlie of the unwritten rules Charlie is violating. His reprimands are like a kindly parental lecture spoken in an even tone, the kind you remember clearly because the words make sense, and the point is never convoluted by the narcissism of temper.

One day, for instance, Lupus calmly emerged from the bedroom to discover Charlie purring on my lap. I was reading and absentmindedly stroking his head. Lupus approached, gently took my hand in his teeth, removed it from the cat, then, using his nose, pushed Charlie off my lap. This accomplished, he turned coolly away, returning to the bedroom as calmly as he had arrived. It wasn't that *he* wanted to be patted, but that Charlie had no business lying on my lap, enjoying my stroking fingers.

Lupus's tolerant affection for Charlie is not inborn; it's a learned trait. I remember the first fall Lupus and I lived in Kingston, barely a month after our return from out west. One night we returned from a coffee klatch downtown, parked behind the house where we boarded, and walked down the dark driveway towards the sidewalk at the edge of the street. Lupus wasn't leashed. As we passed a stand of my landlord's peonies at the edge of the house, I glimpsed a cat hiding among them. Perturbed, I glanced at Lupus, but was relieved when he trotted right by, apparently unaware of the intruding cat, continuing on with me towards the front of the house. As had been asked of us, we didn't walk across the lawn, but waited until we reached the municipal sidewalk before turning up the path leading to the porch. We climbed the steps together and had just about reached the top when, in one fluid motion, Lupus leaped over the porch railing and landed directly in the growth of peonies. The cat barely escaped up a tree in the neighbour's yard. I realized that Lupus had noticed the cat at the same time I had, after all. I'd forgotten how well Lupus could plan a battle or a hunt, how patient he was in setting his traps.

Now that we live with Charlie, I like to think that Lupus would behave differently with the average cat, that he would forgo the cold premeditation he displayed that night in the city. It's not just that Charlie is his friend, as any cat could potentially be, but that Lupus and I are content with ourselves and the life we now share. Back in Kingston, we shared a tension based on our uncertain circumstances. We felt more threatened and defended ourselves aggressively. I'm glad we've left much of that behind us. Lupus and I are calmer, more at peace in the country. We've moved closer to the wilderness, that home that Lupus knows and can teach me to appreciate.

July 1994

I climb the stairs at the front of the house where Lupus and I have been boarding to tell my Kingston landlord that we are ready to leave. We will at last be going. The stairs creak with age in the July heat and each step grows visibly dustier as I ascend. I notice this with a gentle, but familiar, pique. From the very beginning of our residency here, it was agreed that, because I have Lupus with me, I would sweep the downstairs — my own two rooms, the kitchen, and the hallway — at least once a week.

"I'm a neat freak," my landlord said with pride.

Since then, however, I've noticed how clean the downstairs has become, while upstairs, where his bedroom, office/studio and TV room are located, and where, but for visits to the bathroom, I never intrude, the dust and grime continue to accumulate. Over time I've discovered he's not a neat freak at all. More accurately, the person who looks after him must be a neat freak, which isn't the same thing.

I learned such distinctions quite soon after I rented this space from him. As his first boarder, I was told in no uncertain terms how clean the shower must be after I used it. Yet I discovered that, as the landlord, he did not have to clean it at all. I soon decided that none of these ill-tempered demands had much to do with cleanliness; they reflected his need to be in control. I understand control these days. I deal with it in the context of my own evolving life.

And so, after ten months of treading nervously around my landlord's moods, his sudden explosive rages, I am relieved to be moving north of the city. The fact that the rent is half as much only adds to my relief.

I suspect that Lupus is relieved, as well. I've noticed that what bothers me tends to trouble him too. For now, he waits outside in the van I have rented to make this move. It is loaded with the few things we own, the scant possessions we are taking with us as we escape.

At the top of the stairs, I look down the hallway towards my landlord's TV room. I see him sitting on the edge of his sofa, bent over his guitar, half-heartedly strumming a folk song I do not recognize. His mood is morose again. Since we first met, I have found his moroseness oddly intense. While it could be called depression, it can be surprisingly volatile. Even when he is melancholy, he flirts with potential fury. Today is one of those days when his personal pendulum is arcing downwards. Tomorrow it will likely swing upwards again as he accepts the change in his routine my departure represents. He isn't going to miss Lupus and me especially. He'll just miss the comfort and stability of what has been relatively unchanged in the past ten months or so. By tomorrow, though, it will no longer matter to me; I will not have to chart his moods and shape aspects of my life around them.

I haven't told him where I am going. I haven't given him my new landlady's telephone number. This, I have explained, is for his own protection. If he does not know where I am, he cannot find himself ensnared in any moral dilemma. You see, I still have small outstanding bills from a previous life, and gradually I pay them. Gradually is not fast enough for some collection agencies, which call me frequently to accuse me of being a thief and to tell me I should be ashamed of myself. I take debts seriously. All of them will be paid. But it's going to take some time. I hardly make enough money to live.

Barely a month ago, I lost fourteen pounds in two weeks, covering some postdated cheques. I ate rice for two weeks, a loaf of bread, a couple of tomatoes. I sold some records and a few hardcover books so that I did not run out of food entirely. I made sure Lupus had enough to eat before I worried about myself, because I knew he wouldn't understand why we were out of food. Still, he must have noticed how strained we were: we did not go out except for his walks until, at last, some money I was owed arrived to set us free.

Ironically, one of the bill collectors I am now hounded by works for an agency I hired myself less than three years ago. They had little success collecting the money that was owed to me. I told the man on the telephone about his company's failure.

"Were these business accounts?" he wanted to know.

"Yes. I owned a newspaper then."

"It's harder to collect from businesses than it is from people," he admitted readily.

"These were large accounts," I said. Silence on the other end.

"So you see the double standard?" I added, breaking into the void. "One standard for business, another for the working man, the individual?"

"You can look at it that way if you want to," he replied.

"Right now I'm owed eight times the little bit I still owe," I told him so that he could ponder the injustice in this fact.

He paused, but only for a moment. "You have to collect your accounts," was all he said at last.

Now my landlord turns to me as I reach the doorway and stops plucking at the guitar, waiting for me to speak.

"I guess that's it," I tell him. "The truck's loaded. I've swept and vacuumed the place."

"No more Lupus hair?"

"No more Lupus hair. I'll bet you'll be glad to see the end of that."

He shrugs ambivalently.

Last night he watched me pack most of the truck. This morning I awoke early to finish what was left, dismantling and loading the bed, stuffing bedding into new garbage bags before the final cleanup.

"I guess you didn't need my help," he says suddenly, like I've offended him by not asking. It's true I didn't ask. Then again, he didn't offer. He watched me come and go through the front door, carrying a small dresser, a small bureau, my many boxes of books.

"It's done." I don't feel like saying any more.

I still owe him one month's rent, but I have a cheque coming in a couple of days that will cover it. I remind him of this again, stressing that I'll send him his money within the week.

"Okay," he says with a nod. But I know he doesn't believe me.

He reaches for a goblet of white wine that sits sweating nearby on his coffee table. It's not even eleven o'clock. He's starting early today.

I extend my hand. "Thanks for everything," I say politely. I'd like to mean it. Perhaps, in a way, I do.

"We'll probably see you around," he murmurs, after shaking my hand.

"I should think so," I reply, although even this evasion is uttered with a confidence I don't truly feel.

Lupus and I head north out of the city to where we will live in Yarker. He sits upright in the van's passenger seat, his fur rippling gently in the breeze from the open window. I reach across periodically and stroke him behind the ears. We've done this so many times, sharing the front seats of various vehicles while embarking on some expedition or other, hoping to finally arrive some place where we are truly allowed to belong. Our perpetual dislocation creates, yet embodies, the personal paradox that I suspect Lupus and I share: craving the heady charge of rudimentary freedom in making our own choices, yet feeling the need to modify those choices because we can never actually escape the caustic shell of disapproving society.

When we arrive at our destination, I show Lupus the backyard and the woods at the rear, which slope a couple hundred yards down to the river on the lower side of the falls. I point out the shed at the end of the garden, then guide him up onto the back stoop where our rear entrance is located. I try the sliding door there but it is locked, so we wander around to the front.

It's Saturday, and my new landlady is home. She only moved in herself a few weeks before, and she is still enthusiastic about living in the country. I brought Lupus here shortly after she moved in, to examine the rooms he and I will call home. I was pleased to discover the bookshelves already lining the walls. As a writer I shudder whenever most of my books must cower indefinitely inside dusty cardboard boxes. My tenancy here, initially brokered by mutual friends, has taken some time to negotiate, primarily because of Charlie. She fears Lupus will pose a threat to her cat. As part of the negotiation process, we met for coffee in Kingston, then again one evening at her previous home, so that Charlie and Lupus could meet.

Despite this preparation, Lupus and Charlie tend to make strange during our initial few days in the Yarker house. Charlie climbs onto the kitchen cupboards, my landlady's piano, any available high place, to hiss and spit at Lupus, who remains oblivious. He takes no notice of Charlie, and Charlie eventually returns the favour.

Lupus and I settle in. I'm unpacked in less than a day. Lupus finds a favourite spot by the side of my bed. Gradually he develops a range of new habits. After dinner, just before I take him for his evening walk, I ascend the stairs to use the bathroom, and Lupus follows me. He waits outside the door until I'm finished, then, on the way back downstairs, darts in and out between my legs. If I come to a halt on the stairs, he stands there between my legs as if this is a comic routine we've worked out together. If there is an audience, so much the better. Lupus has a sense of humour and can be a bit of a ham. He's been this way as long as I've known him.

On those evenings that I watch a rented video in our small quarters, Lupus lies by the side of the bed until the moment the television goes black. Then, alerted by the sound of it clicking off, he emerges for his last trip outdoors and the dog biscuit that ritually follows.

As the days turn into weeks, we explore this little hamlet, discovering the park on the other side of the river, where we get our exercise each morning and evening.

We do not abandon Kingston entirely, but return fewer than two or three times a week, usually if I am feeling lonely or if we have errands to run that cannot be put off any longer. During our first few months in the country, I feel a conflict between the pull the city exerts over me, and my need to stay away from it. In the city I feel exposed, vulnerable, even hunted in some way. Yet, when I'm away from it for extended periods, I often find that I miss people — strangers in cafés, an acquaintance I might happen upon, some spontaneous exchange of easy conversation.

As time wears on, though, Lupus and I arrange to go to the city less and less. The more I stay away, the less ashamed of myself I am. The less I feel I have somehow failed to meet society's expectations.

For one thing, the calls from bill collectors cease. I am lost to them again, for now at least. Postdated cheques I have written to cover some of my debts are still cashed, a continuing hardship for me, but beyond this I hear nothing.

The week after I send my former landlord the money I owe

him I call to make sure he received it. He is ebullient about its arrival, but he confesses with shameless honesty that he did not think I'd send it. Even his estranged wife told him I would not pay, although it was only one month's rent that was late. I am deeply insulted, but I don't say anything.

"I guess you were right not to tell me where you are," he says.

"Why?" I ask, feeling a familiar uneasiness in the pit of my stomach.

"The sheriff came by two days ago."

"To serve me?"

"I guess so."

"Damn it," I remark. "I don't owe anyone that much money. Did he say who it was for?"

"No. I just told him you'd moved on, that I didn't know where you are. And I don't, do I?"

"No," I murmur.

I hate being pursued this way. I'm doing the best I can. I hate the shame, I hate that I don't have enough money to quickly eliminate the shame. I hate that, historically, money has been so important, the single means to define human value.

"Anyway," my former landlord says, "I'd love to talk some more, but I've got too much to do." He hangs up, leaving me to deal with the humiliation brought on by the news about the sheriff's visit.

The fall is unusually warm, and Lupus and I begin to explore the countryside farther and farther from our new home. We find a small conservation area and systematically hike its limited network of trails. Before winter sets in, I take Lupus to a large area of sand dunes an hour and half by car from where we live. Despite the warm temperatures, extraordinary for late autumn, the dunes are usually deserted. So we wander them freely, gravitating towards the highest ridges we can find. On the summits of the sandy hills, we can look out over Lake Ontario, or turn in the opposite direction towards West Lake, which I know so well from my youth.

My uncle once owned a cottage on West Lake. I can see it in the distance from some of the high dunes here. But my aunt, unable to keep it up, sold it a couple of years after he died. I would have bought the cottage if I'd had the money. She didn't want much for it, but I couldn't afford even the meagre amount she was asking; all my money was tied up with the newspaper I owned at the time. My soul was as tied up in the newspaper as my money was. I even suspected it was slowly destroying me. Gazing at the cottage off in the distance, I realize I'd take Lupus there in a minute, to live there privately. I grew up holidaying or spending weekends at my uncle's cottage. I know it still would have the power to heal most of my wounds.

Despite the twinges of remorse I feel when I glimpse the cottage in the distance, these large, expansive sand dunes, the Sandbanks of Prince Edward County, become our ritual Sunday destination that extraordinary fall. Each week I pack a cooler and we strike out for this destination. Leaving the cooler in the car, we hike to the middle of the dunes to climb one of our favourite hills. Although high winds often blow the sand around, the temperature remains balmy into November. I pin my notebook to my knees against the wind, and I write and write and write. Because no one is watching me and telling me

I shouldn't. Because I am far away from an unforgiving society that deems other pursuits more urgent.

After Lupus and I decide on the spot we'll occupy for the afternoon, I take off his leash. There's never anyone around, little wildlife here to bother, although once he half-heartedly gave chase to a fox, which half-heartedly eluded him. Free of his leash, he can run down to the lake for a drink of water whenever he wants. Lupus likes to wade along the sandy shore. Although he can swim he prefers not to. Instead he leaps high in the air, hopping from spot to spot. I discover he likes to stampede schools of small fish. After they scurry away he stands rigid in the shallows until they gather again. Then he suddenly pounces on them, just to see them flee. These are not challenging fish for him, I know. A skilled fisher, he prefers larger fish in a quickly running stream, not these small fry at the edge of a sandy beach.

Late one November day, when he tires of frightening fish, he returns to lie down beside me. I have brought his tennis ball, and after a while he picks it up off the corner of my blanket, carrying it further up the hill behind me. As I write, the ball whisks down the dune beside me, Lupus silently giving chase. When he snares it again, he patiently carries it back up the hill and the game begins anew. I am used to his tennis ball antics, and I hardly notice as I work on a novel I am writing.

The ball smacks me between the shoulder blades. I turn and glance up the hill. Lupus sits there gazing innocently at some point a few inches over my head. I toss him his ball and return to the sentence he has interrupted.

Smack! The back of my head this time.

I turn. He is innocent. He's looking somewhere else. I stand up, holding the ball in my hand. Suddenly he's coming at me like a rocket. I have a split second to decide to hold my ground, then he takes me out at the knees and down I go on the blanket. All of this happens in silence, muffled by the giving, shifting sands of the dunes and Lupus's ghostly muteness.

As far as I know, animals can't grin. Yet, as I gaze at Lupus looking up the side of the hill at me, I could swear . . .

The November twilight falls quickly. It's nearly dark by the time we return to the car, although it's barely five o'clock. The sudden darkness surprises me in view of the warm temperatures — it feels like September, like the days should be longer. I retrieve our Coleman stove, the charcoal, and starter. I set a picnic table with tin plate, utensils, and condiments, placing Lupus's water and dinner bowls on the grass by an old maple tree. I light a Coleman lamp so that I can see what I'm doing and periodically pump air into it. Lupus curls up on the grass, leashed to a leg of the table, watching me prepare our meal. All of this has become ceremonial for us.

We earn this Sunday feast. For once, we don't have to eat leftovers. Tonight it's an inexpensive cut of beefsteak for Lupus and me, baked potato, broccoli. We make do with less for the other six days of the week, if we are coming here on Sunday, stretching out and sharing large batches of stew or spaghetti, curried dishes with rice that are among Lupus's favourites. Saving up for the occasion enhances our celebration of this day and the evening meal that is its closing rite. The strange, balmy conditions so close to December, this setting with its fine past and finer present, a vague notion that some kind of important wisdom is materializing steadily in the distance — we celebrate all these things on the windswept shores of Lake Ontario.

The place where I prepare our dinner is handy to the car,

and the sand dunes here have given way to rocks and shale. We are on a grassy plateau above a spot where Great Lake winds urge powerful breakers onto the rocks. We have a view of the western sky darkening quickly over the choppy waters. I stand at the table cooking in the developing darkness, the temperature falling rapidly as night moves in on us. I love to cook outside. I love to *be* outside, my flesh accepting dances with elemental courtesans I once denied myself the pleasure of even getting to know.

Each Sunday we spend this way reminds me of our time out west, the months we spent outdoors, trying to be as carefree as we are now. We have no tent to pitch tonight, no campfire to build, but the feeling is familiar, just the same. Not just to me, but to Lupus, too.

I divide my working time between my own writing and book promotion activities, preparing and sending out news releases, setting up launches, interviews, and tours for the publisher who has accepted my first novel, *Too Late The Hunter,* for publication.

Before moving north of the city, I was more engrossed with finding conventional work, but here I give up the search in favour of the freelance activities that, for the time being, are easier to find. When I lived in Kingston, on those occasions that I managed to snare a job interview I was told I was overqualified. I didn't care at the time. I just wanted a job. To pay my debts, to pay my rent, to eat. Perhaps to tell my parents or anyone else who seemed disappointed in the way I live that, yes, I've joined the human race. I'm respectable. I'm employed again.

Still, I failed to find a source for a regular paycheque. And I discovered that even the most menial jobs are presented as careers, requiring a mysterious, nearly spiritual, commitment. I am as perplexed by this unspoken expectation as I am when I am told by a prospective employer that I will probably get bored, or I will want to leave in search of nonexistent greener pastures before they can recoup their investment in me.

So I settle into the inevitability of my situation, concentrating on my freelance work, punctuating it with work on my novel. And, through organization and conservation, Lupus and I manage to survive somehow.

Slowly, hardly aware of it at first, I begin to feel in control of my own fate. I begin to detect a delicate sense of triumph in my personal freedom. Lupus and I are able to structure our days within a framework of balance between responsibility and our own whims. We accomplish not only the work that *must* be done, but also the work we *want* to do. We travel to our favourite haunts, choosing our own destinations, discovering what we wish to discover, avoiding wherever possible what is troublesome or confining for us. We find a haven on the fringes of the punitive society we have recently known, and we achieve this vibrant freedom in relative anonymity. We still take part in life, we don't entirely abdicate, but we find it rewarding to partake of only what we choose.

Lupus settles into our new life as gratefully as I do. He seems not to miss the parks we visited in the city, the various other dogs he encountered there. We begin to insist on spontaneity. We live much more for the moment when we decide to visit the Sandbanks, or travel into Kingston, or hike in the wilderness of Frontenac Park. To us, whim and freedom are necessities that we should encourage in ourselves. Spontaneity reminds us we are vital, and this is one of the most important lessons Lupus teaches me.

I determine one day that I'm less preoccupied with my regrets. The feeling is somewhat like suddenly realizing you've at last recovered from a cold that has hung on for months and months, an infection that's been around so long it's become an accepted part of your normal life. And then, all at once, you notice the symptoms have grown less frequent, that you've nearly recovered.

I suppose this escape from the fierce grip of regret is the initial reward I reap in that first year living north of the city. Not that I consciously decide to give up regret. It's just managed to slip away from me — for the most part, anyway. Regret is like a food I used to nibble at daily, but now, having so many other new things to eat, I've forgotten to include it in my rations.

The regret that slips away from me practically unnoticed during the days and weeks following my departure from the city takes many forms. For instance, there is the regret that I've squandered so much time putting writing on hold to work long hours for conventional goals, predicated upon some fuzzy notion that I should be secure and — more insistently — those I feel responsible for should be secure, as well. Because I have been trained to owe them this obligation of security. There is the regret that I have never found acceptable love, a state of romantic partnership that I did not have to earn by transforming myself into someone conventionally appropriate, someone more acceptable than who I am. And, wedded to this failure, I acknowledge my regret that I have tried for so long to believe in the mythology of romantic love and the idea that I could change myself into whatever I had to in order to fit the mould of this mythology, so rigid, strict, and ritual. Finally, there is the regret that after all my efforts, after so much sacrifice of my time, my health, and the satisfaction of my own needs I have somehow failed to live up to the expectations of both polar axes in my life: mine at the north, everyone else's at the south. The regret that I had been living in some no man's land between my subject and my object, failing both of them, and in the process losing so much of *everything* that I even lost myself.

Regret, I realize, is fading as Lupus and I celebrate a long overdue freedom. But why does this transformation assert itself now? Why at this specific moment in time, given that I've failed to recognize similar opportunities in the past? I have no answers to these questions. There's only Lupus and me, existing in a state of celebration so incrementally realized I hardly notice it taking place. We live impulsively. I am adopting facets of Lupus's character that I do not understand yet. I only sense that life need not have a reason, it need only be alive.

Our autumn celebration is interrupted when I must go to Toronto and then fly on to Nashville on contract for my publisher as part of the work I have been doing to promote an autobiography of a well-known rock musician. Lupus remains behind in the care of my landlady. While I am away, he decides not to forgive me for leaving him behind. Lupus, I have learned, can hold a grudge magnificently.

I'm gone for only eight days. In Toronto, I stay in an expensive hotel, and visit various Toronto television stations with my author: MuchMusic, CBC, and CTV. There's a Canadian launch of the book in a seedy bar downtown, where the musician plays a solo set too good for its humble setting. We fly to Nashville for the American launch. I step into some looking-glass world much different than my own meagre existence and step out of it again eight days later, puzzled at first and disappointed that the escapade is over, then, immediately afterwards, relieved to have regained my freedom.

I can't wait to see Lupus. I've told everyone all about him while I've been away. My landlady brings him to the airport to meet my plane, knowing that I will be glad to rejoin him. It's a rainy night, and cold, more like late autumn should be. As I cross the tarmac towards the gate, I see them waiting in the distance, not far from a wire mesh fence.

When I draw close, Lupus pretends he doesn't know me. I reach down to pat him, but he moves away. To make sure I get the message, he tucks himself in close to my landlady's leg. She asks me how it all went. I tell her that it went well. In unison we glance at Lupus. But he gazes in every direction on the compass to avoid making eye contact with the man who didn't take him along.

"Is he upset because you left him with me?" my landlady asks.

I nod. "He'll be all right in a few days. I'll have to endure some silent treatment first."

"He holds grudges?"

"Yes, he does," I reply wearily.

We drive out of the city towards our home. In between anecdotes and reports on how successful my journey was, I turn and reach out to touch Lupus, but he dances away from my outstretched hand, staring stubbornly at the rain-black windshield and its labouring wipers.

At the house, I carry my suitcase and briefcase to my quarters. After my landlady unhooks his leash, Lupus nearly follows me in. But at the last moment, remembering his grudge, he veers into her living room. I return to stand in her doorway, shaking my head.

"You don't think he's decided to adopt me, do you?" my landlady asks. She and I both know she would never have the patience for an animal like Lupus, at least not beyond the eight days she's spent with him. She's already confessed to me that she enjoys the advantages of cats, finding them more self-reliant. Cats can be left on their own for days at a time, thanks to the convenience of kitty litter and their willingness to subsist on stale cat food and a bowl of lukewarm water.

"Don't worry," I reply. "He just wants to make sure I know that I hurt his feelings."

We stand there studying him, transfixed by his mood and by his ability to clearly convey it.

"Where did he sleep while I was away?" I ask.

"By your bed."

"There you go," I say, and, thanking her again for looking after him, turn and head back into my own quarters. A few moments later, as I'm unpacking my suitcase on the bed, I detect him standing behind me, watching what I'm doing. I turn and crouch. He sits.

"Can't hold out, eh, Loop?" I say uneasily, but hopefully, not daring to feel smug in any way. He's still Lupus: he doesn't wag his tail, there's no overt display of affection on his part. But he's content to sit there and let me rub his chest and stroke him behind the ears. After we make up in this way, he's normal again. And I am deeply pleased he couldn't maintain his distance this time.

This occasion isn't typical. Usually, when Lupus holds a grudge, it's not for minutes or for hours but for *days*. I remember, for instance, camping our way to the West Coast more than a year ago. One day I put his leash on him inside our tent, and as we emerged into the morning sunshine, I tripped over the front flap. As I stumbled, I inadvertently pulled quite hard on the leash, and the chain around his neck tightened with some force. Lupus decided I had done this out of some kind of spite, and no amount of apology or affection could convince him otherwise. What followed was a grudge that lasted for three days. During those three days, I was permitted to feed and walk him but if I approached him to pat him or even merely to talk to him he got up and moved away, throwing himself to the ground with a grunt to let me know he was still annoyed. He grew particularly adept at turning his back on me. I had offended him, and he was not about to let me forget it.

Now, a grudge is not an easy practice to maintain. It takes memory, concentration, and commitment. A grudge has to be nursed even above the instinct to let it go. You have to remember why you're offended and be able to calculate the various means you will use to demonstrate your offence. Holding a grudge takes a good deal of effort, and only a thinking animal will find it worth the trouble. Wrongly or rightly, a grudge requires intellect.

Part of the yardstick I use to measure Lupus's intelligence is the skill and persistence he brings to nursing his hurt feelings. I have believed for a long time that his grudges are one of the indications that Lupus can think, reason, and concentrate. This view of canine intelligence flies in the face of popular theories espoused by many animal psychologists who claim dogs behave only out of instinct, repetition, or a simplistic rationale based entirely on cause and effect. I've read articles promoting this view a number of times. Perhaps, once upon a time, I shared similar assumptions myself. Certainly the dogs I had owned previously gave me no indication that they reasoned sequentially. But Lupus shatters this theory, as far as I'm concerned. I have come to believe that Lupus can think in complex sequences of thoughts.

Still, it has taken me a relatively long time to embrace this conclusion completely. It's not that I don't want to admit an animal like Lupus can plan, but that I am conditioned *not* to believe it. Like not believing in ghosts, I suppose, or in extraterrestrial life, not giving enough credence to serendipity or coincidence. Conditioned by human society to compare my skills and abilities to those around me, thereby to assess my own superiority or inferiority, I may have once assumed the human talent for reasonable thought was less exceptional if animals other than humans were capable of even a rudimentary process that was much the same.

Years ago, though, I happened upon a monkey in a cage at a small private zoo. As I passed, I noticed it was reaching through the bars confining it for a peanut in a shell, which someone had dropped just outside its grasp. I stopped for a moment to watch. After a couple of futile attempts to snare the peanut with its fingers, the monkey reached for a nearby twig and, with great dexterity, used this device to bring the peanut within range. This behaviour, I decided, demonstrated its ability to reason. I could see the sequence of thoughts culminating in the monkey's use of a tool. This was a thought process similar to my own.

As a result, I have come to believe that the ability to reason is evident when an animal is able to organize thoughts sequentially, able to extrapolate that a given action will create an expected result. Organized thought is especially recognizable in certain animals, when the sequence involves more than two distinct components. It might be instinct to detect prey and then stalk it, but it takes thought process to detect prey, set a trap, and then patiently wait for the prey to fall into it.

These conclusions about sequential thought are driven home for me one night as Lupus and I brave a severe snowstorm to go for his nightly walk. I must also return a book to the tiny library in the hamlet where we live. Snowstorm or not, the book is due and, like parking tickets, library fines for a person of my means are an absurd waste of money. By this time Lupus has grown used to me carrying a book to the library every few weeks. If I stop in at the library, which I do on our way back from the park, I leash him to a substantial metal railing just outside the building.

This night is particularly wintry. A brisk wind swirls the falling snow in several random directions. Guided only by the ethereal illumination of streetlights along our route, Lupus and I must stumble down the sidewalk in a grey fog of blustery snow, my right hand clenched at the end of his leash, my left carrying the book I have wrapped in a plastic bag.

On our way to the park we pass the library, which is on the opposite side of the street. Tonight, as we pass, I notice a dog tied to the same metal railing I will tie Lupus to when we return from the park. Bearing in mind that Lupus never misses an opportunity to make the acquaintance of a dog he doesn't know, I am surprised when he ignores the dog across the street, determined instead to continue in the direction of the park. In fact, as we pass the library, he accelerates, virtually dragging me through the accumulating snow with inspired recklessness and strength.

"Hey, Loop, what's the hurry?" I ask as he urges us towards our destination.

Once we enter the park, he drags me through the snow towards a small woods on its boundary, since he prefers to do his business off the beaten track. He does not even give me an opportunity to unleash him. Quickly, he defecates, moves away a step or two, then urinates in one go, oblivious to the territorial route he normally employs. His natural needs completed, he urges me quickly out of the park. By the time we reach the library, I am nearly running to keep up. By now the reason for his behaviour is obvious: he's been hurrying so that he can meet the dog tied to the railing there.

Afterwards, on our way home after meeting the dog—his mission accomplished, his urgency now gone—I consider and eventually marvel at his ability to strategize. The sequence of thoughts, as I examine it, seems remarkable to me: I am carrying a library book and we are therefore going to the library; when he sees the dog already there, we must hurry and do our business so that we can get to the library in time for him to meet the dog. Mere instinct, I realize, would have propelled him across the road towards the library before we gained the park. Reason, however, had already revealed our destination, and told him he'd have an opportunity to meet the other dog. As long as we acted in some haste, that is.

The previous summer, while I sat with Lupus at a downtown sidewalk café, a friend happened along, eating from a tub of ice cream. He decided to share this treat with Lupus and, before I could demur, set the container down on the sidewalk. As we talked, we both grew fascinated by Lupus's approach to eating from this all-too-mobile tub of ice cream. Lupus was leashed to my chair and as he licked the ice cream from the tub it shifted until it sat at the edge of his reach. Then, as if he'd been doing so all his life, he picked the tub up in his teeth and delicately retreated to a spot next to my chair. Then the process began again. The sequence didn't end until he had licked the container clean.

"Where'd he learn to do that?" my friend wanted to know. "Most dogs I know, well, you'd have to do that *for* them."

"I don't know," I replied. "Lupus likes to figure things out for himself."

This stormy night more than six months later, I find myself pondering his ability to organize thoughts sequentially. Is it the dog in him that can think? I wonder. Or is it the wolf? It seems quite clear — to me at least, as I recall occasions when I have seen him hunt — that his reasoning abilities must reside in the part of him that is wolf. I've owned dogs before. None of them could plan. Moreover, none of them could concentrate well enough to hold a grudge for more than a few minutes.

In January my publisher and I sign the contract for my novel. I receive a small cheque to close the deal. And we discuss a biography he'd like me to write a few months down the road.

I want to feel what I should feel: a sense of accomplishment, pride, satisfaction, even joy. I have been writing a long time and have been publishing short stories for more than twenty years. Can I not celebrate the validation that publishing a novel represents? Has the publication of a novel not been my ambition since I was fifteen years old? Can I not now find the courage to say that I am a writer, that the years I spent writing, sprinkled here and there among, and at the permission of, more responsible pursuits, was what I was meant to do? Can I not feel that I was right to want to do so, that this novel indicates a cosmic reason behind the passion motivating me?

Curiously, I feel nothing. I become aware that I'm just too tired, that the validation I should feel has arrived too late. I cannot escape the notion that I have failed. More precisely, I am disappointed by the knowledge that other people will not see my accomplishment as worthwhile. It's not the fact of having my novel published that has let me down, but that it won't matter to anyone else. I still do not possess the private courage, the self-sustainability, to care on my own, without requiring someone else's approval. No wonder I am tired. I begin to realize that my life has been an apology for much too long. Being sorry is a hard habit to break. I can't just expect to stop feeling inadequate now I feel that my life seems to have achieved some of its inevitable purpose, some acceptable justification.

Lupus is waiting for me in the car, sitting behind the wheel, when I return from signing the contract. He moves to the passenger seat as I climb inside.

"You see this, Loop?" I say, holding the document up. "He's publishing my novel, probably in the fall."

But my best friend doesn't react, of course. Perhaps he could understand if I felt the joy I need to feel, but without this necessary emotion, all he can comprehend are a few scruffy sheets of paper and the wan inadequacy of my emotionless words.

I insist to myself that I should celebrate. My landlady is home when Lupus and I get back later that afternoon. I tell her I've signed the contract and invite her to share a glass of wine with me. I reach into my cupboard and retrieve a bottle of Valpolicella I have been saving for many months. For an occasion like this, I suppose.

She's polite enough to toast my success and drink two glasses with me. Then she must cook herself an early dinner before heading into the city for a get-together she plans with friends. But this brief celebration of my news doesn't accomplish much for me, doesn't cause my constricted pleasure to expand into true celebration. In the end, I think both of us simply feel awkward.

Anyway, the people who would share my triumph aren't here to help me unearth my joy. Either they've gone away already, or I haven't found them yet. At this time in my life, I know too many people who I'm convinced have already *decided:* what success is, and what failure is, what we all deserve, what matters in this world. Conventional and judgmental, they firmly believe a novel is none of these.

But maybe over time my success with the novel will become more real. Maybe who I am and what I want to do and how it might all work out will come clear at some point in the unforeseeable future. Maybe it just takes time. Time to undo the damage that has been done by living an inauthentic, dishonest life. Time to discover the strength and self-reliance necessary to decide what matters most all by myself, without anyone's endorsement.

The wine, as a celebration at least, is clearly a waste. I won't drink the rest of it on my own. In the end, I use it in a recipe or two, practical to the end, not consuming it in quite the way I had initially intended.

"Nook? Is that you?" a plump woman says early one afternoon, noticing, then studying Lupus where he lies in the shade of a tree on a friend's lawn. Lupus glances at her, bored and aloof, then turns away again. The woman tugs on the arm of someone she is with and points at Lupus. "Doesn't that look like Nook? Don't you think so?"

But the other woman has come to this garage sale to shop and explore, not to gaze at snoozing dogs. She just shrugs and moves off along the asphalt driveway where one of my friends sells a variety of goods to help herself survive.

We are in Kingston, where most of the people I know are nearly as poor as I am. I suppose we end up knowing each other because there are so many places we cannot go, so few places we can afford to be. People of similar means fall into ghettos which bring us together—we're all sorted by attrition, like little bits of wilted spinach not good enough to be tossed into the salad.

The woman who conducts these sales on her parents' driveway shares a mutual friend with me, an artist who's depressed, who can't quite understand how he fell on hard times. He's in Canada's *Who's Who,* but he's also on welfare; no one will give him a job. Yet I was with him one day when he brought a coffee and a bagel for a homeless man. I've noticed a pattern in who looks out for whom. Those of us who are poor try to help one another whenever we can. The times demand it.

It's late June now, crisply sunny, one of those days that crackles. My friend is doing a roaring trade. I show up most weekends to see how she's doing and to catch up on the news. Sometimes, if I have a little spare money, I'll buy something I think I need, a coffee mug or a couple of plates. A ten-pin bowling ball once, for which I coughed up a dollar. Eventually I sold it to someone for the same price. I haven't been bowling since young adulthood and the ball, a purple and pink monstrosity, was marred by nicks and scratches. I guess getting rid of it without taking a loss can be construed as good fortune.

"Is he your dog?" the plump woman asks me.

I've been sitting on the front steps in the shade, some distance from the tables at the sale, thinking I should be going. I stand up and tell her, yes, he's mine.

"He looks like a dog I used to have. I called him Nanook."

Something in me wants to groan. Did she say Nanook?

"Nook? Is that you?" she asks again.

"I call him Lupus," I say.

Lupus gets up, stretches, then settles himself again on the cool grass in the shade. The woman, as far as *he's* concerned, does not exist. She can stand there all day long, he'll never give her a moment's notice.

He's always behaved this way. I'm no longer embarrassed by this aloofness in him. When Lupus wants attention, he lets you know. Otherwise, you're wasting your time.

"God, it's *got* to be him," the woman says. "Where'd you get him?"

"The Humane Society," I say. "About two and half years ago."

"It *is* him, isn't it? I took Nook to the Humane Society." Before she can run the risk of having me ask her why, she adds,

"Does he like Milkbone dog biscuits?"

"You bet."

"Does he run your deer?"

"If he can," I say.

"Oh, Nook," she says. Then she glances at me again. "He looks good. He looks happy."

"Yeah, I think so," I reply.

"The man I lived with, my boyfriend, didn't like him. I took him to the pound just to hear the end of it. Now I wonder if I should have taken my boyfriend to the pound instead."

I smile.

This is the day I finally learn where Lupus came from. The plump woman tells me about his family tree and how he wandered out of the woods one day, mostly wild, when he was just a pup. I've already learned how much wolf he is (something I discovered while we were out west) but this last piece in his specific puzzle is gratifying to know.

"Does he give you any trouble?" she asks.

"Not really," I reply.

"God, he looks good."

She turns to Lupus, considering him for another moment, then seems to gather herself together. "I'm glad it worked out for you, Nook," she tells him at last.

He just ignores her.

I shrug, faintly awkward that he doesn't acknowledge this moment as dramatic in any way. Then again, maybe it's *not* dramatic, and he's the superior one because he knows it's not.

She grins, at Lupus, perhaps, or because she's reading my mind.

A moment later, she's gone.

January 1994

Our first winter back from out west is a harsh one. Lupus and I settle into the rented rooms in Kingston and begin to embark on what I think of as some kind of recuperative life. I consider our current mission a prickly amalgam of getting over our losses and finding the path that leads us back to something acceptable again. *Something* on good days, *anything* on bad days. I still feel the need to fit into conventional society, to smother the conflict assimilation creates in me. Sometimes fitting in seems like the only available option. At other times I wonder if doing so is ultimately pointless. I'm still preoccupied by what I've recently lost. Some losses are so complete they seem incomprehensible, as if they're too much for our cognitive grasp. I've lost so much recently, a home, a business, a romantic partner, it feels like *everything* is gone. Throw in the loss of the good health I once took for granted and the persistent suspicion that the person I used to be isn't the person I want to be at all, and, yes, one could conclude that my losses amount to just about everything.

I persevere, trying to be useful, trying to regroup, putting the various pieces of my life back together again. I still believe that by shaping myself into some conventional mould I can somehow make everything all right. If I do the "right" thing persistently enough, perhaps I can smother the nagging notion that I am capitulating. Or if I can't smother it, perhaps it will drift away like any other fanciful notion. Perhaps I'll forget that going west was intended to be a spiritual quest, a rebirth, a flaunting of my newfound freedom before the smug, faceless audience of social acceptance. Perhaps I'll conclude that Lupus and I would not have returned if our quest was meant to succeed. Then I'll no longer wonder if we gave up on it because freedom was obfuscated by an unexpected loneliness I found mysteriously frightening.

For now I cling desperately to what is familiar and resolve not to deviate from the accepted way of doing things. A conventional life is the right one. It must be. Virtually everyone on the planet clings to this idea unquestioningly, apparently having decided conventionality is the only option that yields any permanent value. If so many adhere to it, the conventional path must have true merit. This is what I tell myself, at least.

Yet I am nagged by the possibility that conventionality has no true merit, in which case I must conclude that many millions of people do not know themselves or what they truly want from life. And that would mean the world is crazy. If so, I guess I'm not ready to accept it yet. And if I ever did accept the notion that millions of my fellow humans were willfully self-deluded, I'd have to find a courage so new and rich it would compel me to relegate conventional life to the back burner where, sometimes, I still suspect it belongs.

Then again, there is Lupus. He seems to know an essential truth about living that I have not fully accepted. I catch glimpses of this knowledge in his speed and curiosity, his sense of adventure, his talent for pure being. But, although I recognize these things in Lupus, I don't understand them intimately enough to embrace them in my own life. He enjoys an adventure in his days and a basic acceptance of himself that I can hardly fathom in mine.

While we were travelling out west, I noticed Lupus's relationship to nature, the way it accommodated him and the way he accommodated it. I caught glimpses of his sense of place in the outdoors, the way, on a nature trail, as we hiked, his enjoyment of sensation seemed enjoyed purely for sensation's sake. Spirited runs, brief physical challenges — these seemed to be a celebration of being alive. Most of the time these moments were forgotten not long after I recognized them, but I detected them nonetheless, imagining that I could someday learn to be motivated by whatever carefree self-actualization drives Lupus. Now that we've returned, these brief impressions of Lupus's confident freedom — and how it is achieved — have dimmed significantly.

Having returned to the city, I feel again the incipient terror of life. I am aware again of how vast and complex conventional existence can be, swarming with thousands of minute details that one must swat to death each day.

I see Lupus approach life in a way that D.H. Lawrence would have approved of, namely being "red in tooth and claw." The minutiae preoccupying my life when I was gainfully employed provided no time for the pursuit of a private, passionate life. It was a weird world of missing paperclips, jammed photocopiers, telephone tag. No wonder I feel terror at the prospect of returning to normalcy. If I am unable or unwilling to learn what Lupus knows instinctively then I will remain mired in tragic disappointment while life passes me by.

January. The temperature has stayed well below zero for nearly two weeks. And it's been snowing despite the frigid temperatures, unusually deep accumulations piling up along the sides of the roads. For days my landlord and I have been listening to the crunchy squeak of snow complaining under our boots as we deliver thousands of bulletins and reports I've prepared for the government of the township immediately east of Kingston. I've hired my landlord to help me with the delivery. Although he collects unemployment insurance, he maintains he needs the money nearly as much as I do. And I need his help to complete the project on time.

On the surface it seems that my landlord and I have things in common: no regular employment, a desperation to recapture the conventional approval we once enjoyed, and an idea that, through diligence and perseverance, we can get everything we've lost back, thereby silencing the vindictive voice in both our minds telling us to be ashamed of ourselves. Neither of us affixes any blame for our discontent on the external world. We are both certain that the fault for any perceived lack in our characters resides solely within ourselves. Although we don't verbalize it, each of us is privately convinced that if we can only reinvent ourselves along more conventional lines we can force life's relentless merry-go-round to slow down a little, and we'll hop on board again, our inadequacies forgiven. Neither of us admits we want to seek conventional approval.

Sometimes, when we are embarking on our day together, my landlord laments the menial nature of what we are doing, striding from door to door with bundles of printed matter.

"You mean you feel ashamed?" I want to know.

"Embarrassed, anyway," he admits. "I want a good job again, my old life back, when I felt like I was a success."

I consider his words in silence.

"Don't you feel the same way?" he asks.

"I feel it," I admit, "but not as much as you do. There's a side of me that wants to step back from the conventional definition of success. I'm suspicious we're inventing what we want to go back to."

"Inventing it?"

"Maybe conventional success or respectability is inauthentic."

"Crap," my landlord says.

Most of the time, though, we work together with hardly a word, the bundles of municipal memoranda and regulations in the trunk of my car evaporating piece by piece as we drive endless rural routes and walk through hastily constructed suburbs, tucking the materials into mailboxes.

Lupus occupies the back seat of my car, sometimes resting his chin on a bundle of paper beside him. My landlord is perplexed that I take Lupus with us, but Lupus is willing to endure long hours in the car to be with me.

"Besides," I protest, "you don't want me to leave him at home where he can chew on the furniture, do you?"

My landlord tolerates Lupus but doesn't understand our relationship. As long as I clean up his fur balls and keep my word about not letting him into the backyard garden when summer comes, Lupus will be no trouble. That's what my landlord wants from Lupus: he wants him to be trouble-free. Never mind appreciating him or deriving pleasure from his unusual qualities the way so many other people do.

My landlord, I've determined, is too busy fretting about his own life, which consists mostly of a long list of needs that must be met and the anger that flares up each time he experiences a minor setback, to have time for an animal like Lupus. Besides, he's already told me about the dog he used to have with his wife and daughter. He came home from work one day after it had grown old and sick and, deciding enough was enough, took it to the vet to terminate its misery. He neglected to discuss this decision in advance with his family. He just went ahead with the execution on his own, leaving his wife and daughter with no opportunity to say goodbye to their pet. His unilateral action became another in the long list of reasons his wife had for desiring that their marriage come to an end.

I hear stories like this when his ex-wife comes over for dinner. Sometimes we talk after my landlord has gone upstairs to nap on the couch in his TV room, succumbing to the white wine he consumes each day, his blond hair in disarray, his blue eyes glazed with wine. As marital dissolutions go, I find their estrangement puzzling. She not only visits on a regular basis, but he sometimes stays overnight at her apartment. "Not having sex," he points out, but locked in some lonely, ambivalent embrace that is less about love than about fearing to face failure or getting on with life. I sense that they can't hang on and they can't let go. They even maintain a domestic facade for some of their friends and relatives, still attending functions as a married couple and adopting the familial role that their particular circle seems to expect or demand. Their relationship has nothing to do with happiness. It has more to do with habit, and some need to cling to the tattered threads of familiarity.

And there I am, caught in the middle of their ambivalence. I find it difficult sharing a kitchen and bathroom with a housemate for whom so much is over and not over, for whom so much remains unclear and unresolved. My landlord's lack of resolution seems to have a determination all its own. Do people prolong their suffering simply because it is familiar, or because something malignant in their souls derives enjoyment from it? I try not to judge my landlord and his ex-wife, but try instead to remember if I once behaved this way myself. And if I did, what adjustment can I now make so that I don't repeat my past mistakes?

During these first months back in Kingston, for his exercise each day I take Lupus to the municipal park and racetrack up the street from where we live. Here he gets to meet new canine playmates on a regular basis and be admired by their masters. He soon enjoys a notoriety based on his astonishing physical prowess. Recognizing his ability to draw attention to himself, he shows off shamelessly. I ignore that part of my human sensibility that tells me I should be embarrassed by his immodesty.

"Lupus has wheels," a young man tells me one evening that winter, when we meet at the track to exercise our animals.

"Yes, he does," I say.

We've been watching our dogs play and cavort. But his dog, short-legged and plump, can't hope to keep up under these winter conditions. Lupus runs nearly as fast in deep snow as he does on bare ground.

"You ever clocked him?"

"Once," I reply. "Last year on a country road near where I lived. I chased him down the road in my car. He was doing sixty clicks an hour."

The young man whistles.

Because of his speed, Lupus has a preference for certain breeds of dogs as playmates. He likes German shepherds or hounds because they are usually quite fleet and can almost keep up. And these dogs are more willing than others to play his favourite game: Chase Lupus. The object of Chase Lupus is to run from your pursuers as fast as you can, all the while enticing them to try to cut you off. As pursuing dogs close in by cutting down the angles, Lupus likes to leap over them at the last minute, escaping at full speed. His leaping ability is as profound as his running speed, and he employs it whenever he can to enhance his pleasure in play. I am used to his predisposition for taking flight. He has always delighted in standing beside my right leg, then, without warning, soaring up to nip the top of my shoulder.

On occasion, I fear he will injure himself in his exuberance. One day at the racetrack, after I release him from his leash and he dashes into the centre of the oval, he performs a stunt that fills me with alarm. It is late February, and we have enjoyed a thaw that's lasted several days, melting most of the snow. But now it is cold again and, here and there, large patches of treacherous ice have formed, lurking on the brown surface of winter turf. As Lupus runs flat out across the oval, I notice he is headed for one of these large expanses of ice. I know, if he hits it at full speed, he could injure himself, perhaps breaking a leg. But before I can cry a warning, he casually leaps this large sheet of ice, stretching out in a classic, soaring glide. Upon landing, he continues on his way at breakneck speed.

While he sniffs the territory around the backstops and bleachers of the nearby baseball diamonds, I cautiously pace the slippery sheet of ice he crossed in mid-air. Twenty-eight feet. I am astonished not only by the length of his leap, but by the ease and self-assurance with which he accomplished it. I find myself envying his self-confidence. What compromising doubts must one shrug off to believe in one's abilities so completely?

The following May, Lupus enjoys the company of a hound named Zeus, one of his favourite playmates. Their game takes them to the top of a steep rock cut. The sheer drop is twelve to fifteen feet, but he keeps going anyway, arriving at the edge and soaring off it without missing a step. When he lands safely at the bottom, he continues running until he comes to a halt a few feet from where I stand. Panting with exertion and pleasure, he glances at me coyly, in search of an expression of admiration.

"Holy shit!" mutters Zeus's master beside me.

Soberly I nod. "I wish he wouldn't do things like that. I keep thinking he's going to end up hurt."

Zeus refrains from attempting the same stunt. Instead he descends the rock cut in the same location where he and Lupus first climbed it.

Later I wonder which of Lupus's characteristics came first: his joy and zeal or his physical prowess? If one has a certain self-esteem, does ability rise to meet it? Or is it the reverse? And, in Lupus's case, where does his confidence originate? Is it his love for life or his ability to resist doubt that nurtures his glee and intrepidity?

Lupus's desire to socialize with other dogs is new. More than a year ago, when we lived in the country east of Kingston, Lupus rarely had the opportunity to meet other dogs. Nor was there much opportunity to do so on the journey we took out west after living east of Kingston, since we were too often on the move. I am relieved to discover he enjoys the company of dogs, although at times there are some anxious moments.

One day, as we are about to leave the racetrack to go home, he meets a Labrador retriever pup only a few weeks old. The retriever, a miniature collection of clumsy tumbles, buckling legs, and boundless enthusiasm, charges at Lupus to play. I feel an instinctive nervousness. Although Lupus is barely three years old himself, he hasn't shown much patience with immature dogs, favouring playmates that are closer to his own age. I worry that this clumsy and insistent retriever, not old enough to know when his antics might not be appreciated, will annoy him. Lupus is on his leash; at the first sign of trouble I will pull him away.

But Lupus displays a profound affection towards this canine infant. He lies down on the grass to let the younger dog nip at his face, belly, and feet. His willingness to be accommodating surprises me, he has always been so aloof. With great patience he lets the pup climb all over him. I am relieved and amused as it tumbles clumsily onto the grass, gets up, and wades in again. Lupus's display of parental affection fills me with admiration.

Eventually the tiny retriever and its master must depart. As they labour across the field, I notice Lupus following their progress with a wistful gaze. Finally he performs his version of an accepting shrug, and we slowly turn away and leave resignedly for home.

Despite his general sociability, I am still cautious whenever Lupus and I encounter dogs we do not know. The dog in his nature is relatively predictable, but the wolf in him responds quite viciously to trouble. Although he is never aggressive, deflecting unwanted attention with aloof disdain, when he is attacked he defends himself with a violence and skill I find disturbing.

His intensity was made apparent to me at the racetrack when he encountered an aggressive shepherd. We were on our way home, about to walk through the open gateway, when the shepherd dashed around the corner of a nearby building, its master several yards behind. Unleashed, the shepherd raced towards Lupus, growling and snarling. Lupus submitted, lying down on his back and exposing his belly to the larger dog, the way wolves sometimes do when they're obeying the code that maintains their pack hierarchy.

The shepherd, apparently unaware of the significance of

Lupus's gesture, bit him on the lower chest. Before I could pull Lupus away, he was up, still connected to his leash, battling this larger dog. In seconds he had torn off flesh and fur from areas around his adversary's genitals, apparently intent on disembowelling him. I pulled Lupus away quickly. The shepherd, crying out in pain, wisely retreated. Its owner, arriving on the scene furiously silent, leashed his injured dog. There wasn't much he could say in the end; he'd witnessed the entire incident. We stood there awkwardly, assessing the damage, muttering various apologies, then led our animals away.

As Lupus and I walked home, I discovered I was trembling.

Late spring now. Taking advantage of the warmer weather, Lupus and I explore other parks in the city. On this particular day, we walk several blocks down to the waterfront. There, I leash Lupus to my belt so that we can sit down and enjoy the shade from a maple's thick foliage. The large park is crowded with tourists out for a stroll and other people walking their dogs. Everyone behaves themselves. All the dogs are leashed and, as if by tacit agreement, we give each other a wide berth. All of us are careful in case our animals grow quarrelsome.

A short time later, a large Rottweiler suddenly intrudes on this peaceful setting. I hear it coming before I actually see it. I have just enough time to get to my feet, Lupus still leashed to my belt, before the Rottweiler charges. There are no preliminaries. The big dog attacks without warning. The encounter is brief but fierce. The Rottweiler sustains significant injuries to its throat and neck before it concludes it should retreat. I am helpless during the battle. To pull Lupus away could leave him defenceless. At the same time, until the Rottweiler retreats, I am caught in the middle of the two combatants, one of whom is leashed to my belt. I know it takes only seconds, but it seems much longer than that before the young man to whom the Rottweiler belongs arrives on the scene. He leashes his animal as I pull Lupus away.

"Jesus," he says, "look at my goddamned dog."

I do. It has been cut in several places around the neck. Bits of bloodied fur lie on the ground. After a closer examination, I am relieved to conclude that the injuries look more serious than they actually are.

"My dog is leashed," I say without sympathy. "This is a public park. You should leash your fucking dog, especially when he's aggressive like that."

A crowd has now gathered and most of them have witnessed the disturbance. I hear them murmuring in agreement with my stern response. The Rottweiler and its owner have no basis for argument. And Lupus, whether deviously or not, has now sat down by my leg as if little of what has just transpired had anything to do with him.

"What kind of dog fights like that?" the young man protests feebly before he turns away.

"A dog on a leash that is attacked by a bigger dog that isn't," I reply with a calm I do not feel.

The murmurs of assent from around me are enthusiastic; they even approach the verge of scattered applause. The young man and his Rottweiler are relieved to withdraw. But I find myself trembling again. While I am pleased Lupus can defend himself with skill, I detest violence of this kind. For his part, Lupus merely lies back down in the shade, the incident now apparently forgotten.

I think, in many cases, dogs become what their human masters wish them to be. While specific breeds are prone to certain behaviour or have certain aptitudes, skills, and characteristics (most golden retrievers I've met are placid, the three Dalmatians I've encountered all tried to bite) most dogs will be encouraged to behave in the ways their masters expect them to. Usually human expectations of dogs reflect an individual's attraction to one breed over another, which is based, more often than not, on the perceived qualities that a given breed possesses. Rottweilers and pit bull terriers are attractive to some because of their reputation for fierceness, and whatever is innate in them to make them potentially nasty is often encouraged. Although I've met friendly and passive Rottweilers or pit bulls on a number of occasions, there are people who are attracted to these dogs because they *want* them to be aggressive. Which is unfortunate for those animals in particular and the resulting reputations of their breeds in general.

Later that same spring. Lupus and I have been down at the lakefront and are returning home. It's hot and sunny, and we are tired after a pleasant outing. As we pass a sidewalk patio adjacent to a restaurant a couple of blocks from where we live, I notice two stocky men sitting at a table, drinking beer in the afternoon sunshine. They are heavily tattooed, rough, bearded, and unkempt. Approaching them, I do not notice the two pit bull terriers with them, arrayed in studded collars and lounging in the shade underneath the table, connected to their respective leashes. As Lupus and I pass, the two dogs suddenly attack through the patio railing, startling both of us. Without breaking stride, Lupus, snarling viciously in response, feints at the two dogs. Unused to the ferocity of his response, the pit bulls race back under their table, terrified. No blood or physical injury this time — the leashes, the railing, and our hurry to be gone prevent any true altercation. In fact, the disturbance is all over and done in seconds. The pit bulls evaporate in silence. Lupus trudges on towards home, and I feel awash in profound relief.

The two men behind me make no remark. I also say nothing. The silence between us is thick. Yet, a yard or so later, I cannot resist glancing over my shoulder at the two unapologetic men. When I do, I discover them staring at Lupus and me, their mouths open, clearly dismayed that their dogs were driven back.

Caricatures, I decide later, these two men and their dogs.

I sit in the riding office of an Ontario provincial member of Parliament, awaiting an interview. Although it is only late May, the day is extraordinarily hot and humid. The air conditioner hums just above the front door, and I am grateful for it. This office is barely three blocks from where Lupus and I board, and I have walked to keep my appointment, a decision I now regret. Dressed in slacks, a tie, and a sport jacket, I feel sticky with sweat, the fruits of my exertion.

The job I'm here to interview for is only part-time, mostly light office work, but I have high hopes I'll get it. Much of my freelance work has disappeared in the past few months, and I still crave the security a more permanent position would provide. As I wait to be ushered into the MPP's office, I consider how our past association should give me an advantage, especially since the position I'm applying for is not demanding. Six years ago, before he was elected, he interviewed me on the cable television program he had at the time. This was during the 1988 federal election, and I was a candidate for his party in the riding next door. Following my defeat in the federal election, I consulted with his team on their media campaign, before he was elected in 1990. Not only have we battled for the principles of the same party, but he is familiar with my skills and work ethic. And I believe he'll understand how desperately I need a job.

When at last I'm called into his private office, I find three people waiting for me. The MPP has been joined by his riding office manager and a representative from Queen's Park. My political colleague wastes no time telling me that my abilities exceed the requirements of the position. I have barely sat down before he announces that I'm overqualified.

Before I can reply, the man from Queen's Park adds, "Your resumé reflects a more demanding position. You should be an executive assistant to a cabinet minister, as far as I'm concerned." He lists a few items from my resumé to support his view.

"If you have an opening, I'm available," I say good-naturedly, hoping I don't sound glib or brash. But he doesn't have any openings for executive assistants.

The problem, they explain, is that the job I've applied for is just a part-time office job. They take such great pains to explain this to me, I wonder why they bothered to interview me at all.

"In view of your history with the party, the work you've done before, we felt we owed you the interview," I am told, as if they've been reading my mind.

"I see."

"You must see our dilemma."

I hesitate, biting back a deep frustration. "Here's *my* dilemma," I say. "I have no job, and I have no money. Sometimes food is a luxury. I'm qualified for positions that aren't open and overqualified for some that are. Freelance projects come and go . . . these days they mostly go. To be blunt, I can't eat the accolades in my resumé. They don't pay the rent."

They are sympathetic but unyielding. They digress for a few moments to compliment me on the editorial quality of the newspaper I ran before circumstances forced me to close its doors.

"What happened there, anyway?" the member of the legislature wants to know.

I tell him about the thousands of dollars in delinquent accounts, the exhaustion of trying to collect them, the difficulties keeping the newspaper going and maintaining my physical health.

"That's right, you were in hospital, weren't you?"

"Yes," I reply.

"You have a lot of media experience, especially in newspapers."

I nod.

"Actually my media person mentioned he was concerned you'd be looking over his shoulder."

"Not if he doesn't want me to," I reply. "I don't poke my nose where it doesn't belong. I just want a job. I just want to eat."

Silence. I get nowhere. Having time to waste, they have wasted mine.

It's the last job interview I will put myself through. The pattern is always the same. I cannot convince anyone that extra qualifications are a bonus for an employer when he can obtain them cheaply. No one considers that to neglect to take advantage of extra qualities is foolish. Instead of recognizing the value in a bargain, they feel threatened by it.

By that evening, as Lupus and I sit outside in the quickly waning heat of the day, I conceive of changing direction. First of all, I must cut my losses, reduce the cost of my rent, and buy myself more time to seek out freelance work. Writing is what I do and writing is how I will have to make my living. There's only Lupus and me. It seems clear that now is the right time to live life *my* way, outside the tragic vacuity of a society that doesn't have the imagination to include a place for me.

Hungry times, I know, will follow this decision. But a hungry belly, I am beginning to realize, is more endurable than a hungry spirit. I sense that I have turned some important corner in my life, that I am ready to dare to be myself.

In a mood of ambivalent defiance and trepidation, I sit on the porch with Lupus that evening, coming to my conclusions. Thinking our respective thoughts, we watch the sun go down, watch the streetlights come on. My decision to live life authentically is a matter of imagination, my imagination, the courage to defy. Society cannot so easily crush someone with enough imagination to live life by his own rules.

September 1993

We're in Alberta in the year of my despair and disappointment. I am in this part of the country because the spiritual quest I embarked on two months ago has sputtered to a futile end. The sense that my adventure is suddenly over is so profound, it feels like it never even got started. Endings can be that way, looming so massively and formidably they crush even the recollection of their innocent beginnings. Or is today's conclusion merely the faint echo of a failure already suffered three weeks ago, the day Lupus and I drove east out of the splendour of the Rocky Mountains? It felt like the geography itself was evicting us then, casting us out as fools.

It's close to the end of September. The sky above this Calgary suburb is overcast. I expect it to rain again. It rains too much here, and it's too chilly for a man like me. Everyone complains about the weather out here — on street corners, lined up at cash registers — yet they stay here anyway, committed to their jobs or their families, I suppose.

Even though it's relatively early on Sunday morning, my brother and his family have risen to say goodbye to us. I uttered my farewells and thank yous the previous night, but I suppose it's more proper to do so closer to the gaping precipice of our departure. Maybe it's just Lupus that everyone wants to bid farewell to. They've come to like him a great deal in the past three weeks. He inspires affection in people. Even though he's aloof and independent, it's easy to fall in love with him.

I'm more difficult, I expect, like a particularly complex bomb no one quite knows how to defuse. And I feel so confused these days, I'm sure people cannot help but wonder why they would even take the trouble trying to figure me out. The confused and misdirected have a welcome place in our society — those more "stable" members look to us with a sense of smug superiority. But the confusion can become pretty tiresome should someone get too close to it.

My brother asks if I have enough money to get back to eastern Ontario. I tell him I think so. But it's going to be close. I have a couple days' food and I've filled the car with expensive Alberta gasoline. I have $160 remaining in my wallet to take me more than two thousand miles. I've made my calculations. If we spend only one night in a campground, I should just be able to make it back.

So we say our farewells. I thank everyone again. Will I return in the near future? "I don't know," I say. "Depends on what's happening when I get back."

It's not so much a drive as an endurance test. Crossing a generous portion of Canada's landscape as quickly as possible, Lupus and I in retreat, heading east, back to where this journey began a couple of hopeful months ago. Call my feelings apprehension, call them quiet panic. Whatever, our desperation means pointing the car in an easterly direction, then hanging on for dear life, trying not to think too much about how futile it seems to be, heading back to the place we thought we'd left behind.

I suppose I'm looking for something familiar, something safe, giving up on my vague concept of freedom because it just seems too nebulous, too incomprehensible, too inherently fugitive for me to embrace it after all. Nearly out of money, nearly out of hope, nearly out of reasons.

"Sorry, Lupus," I say, feeling the need to apologize. It's clearly my fault we're going home with our tails between our legs. In my mind, I'm the one letting both of us down. Freedom is just too difficult.

I'm returning to Ontario to reconnect with the woman who was my partner, who refused to join me out west. A romantic imperative, I guess. I have to know for sure if she is lost to me. Yet I feel foolish and inadequate. I never expected that she would slip away from me. It was everyone else, it seems, that somehow expected it.

In the car I unfasten Lupus's leash. He must sit in the passenger seat because the back seat, like the trunk, is jammed to capacity. Still, we aren't taking anything back that we didn't bring out west with us. I'm fully aware that I haven't gained or lost a thing over the past two months. Except the relationship that may have disappeared in Ontario while I was away.

"Well, Loop," I say, before I start the car, "here we go again." He doesn't seem to object. Sometimes I wish I could be like him.

I fuel up in Regina later that afternoon. I can feel bad weather coming. As I pump gas at a self-serve, the wind gusts so powerfully I fear it will blow me out of the service station lot, carrying me like Dorothy to some inhospitable Oz.

"Something's coming," I say to the pierced young man in the booth who takes my money.

All he says is, "Yup."

I realize I'm just one more hapless Ontarian drifting across his mysterious prairie. People like me come and go, I suppose, while he is rooted here.

We drive on. I stop periodically so Lupus can relieve himself, but most of the time he refuses. He's been this way consistently during the thousands of miles we have travelled recently, not drinking, not urinating. He likes to save all of these functions until we reach a destination, travelling light, like we're on some determined lupine mission and must deprive ourselves until we finally accomplish it.

Mostly he curls up on the front seat beside me, compacting himself into a tight ball. Lupus is a changeling. He fluctuates between being small and large to suit his circumstances, adapting himself to the place he must fit or the character he must convey when he's confronted by an enemy or a friend. At times he appears to be a dog, but he changes when he must into something longer, faster, and meaner, something clearly wolf.

He naps as we speed along the Trans-Canada. Then, each

time he hears the rhythmic click of my signal light, he sits up on the seat, wondering if this means we're now going to stop. If we keep moving, he settles down again, philosophical about going on, curled dozing into the tight ball the narrow space requires of him.

I was right about the weather. By the time we stop that night, about an hour before midnight, the temperature has dropped well below zero. We've found a private campground that is still open for the season, and I pitch our tent deep in its interior, battling blowing snow and treacherous winds, stopping to warm my hands when they begin to ache but too busy to root through the trunk for the gloves I vaguely remember packing a couple of months ago. I can hardly believe this is only the end of September. I'm astonished by this ferocious, premature arrival of winter.

Lupus curls up on the grass while I cook dinner. The blowing snow collects on his fur and in the crevices between his body and the ungiving ground, but he covers his face with his tail and doesn't seem to mind. I stand inside the gale, stirring a pot of simmering leftover homemade stew, watching snowflakes dive and leap into the pot, white lemmings throwing themselves over the cliff into our meal.

While I cook, I use a Coleman heater to warm up my tent and sleeping bag, turning it off for safety reasons when we finally retire. The air is soon cold again. I put on a toque and huddle deep into the sleeping bag. Lupus remains in his curl on his blanket beside me. Outside, the wind wails and slaps at our tent. We both sleep soundly anyway.

Next morning we're up early. We find three or four inches of snow on the ground and discover that the fierce overnight winds have blown down tree limbs and branches. The wreckage lies broken all over the landscape, frozen twigs cling to the canvas roof of our tent. It remains cold, well below zero. I remark on this to Lupus because it still surprises me. "I feels like January, Loop, not the end of Septemember," I remark.

I dig out some winter supplies I brought with us: a goose-down coat, gloves, another toque, extra shoes. When we left Ontario at the end of July, I didn't know how long we'd be out west. For once my uncertainty has rewarded me, and I am actually prepared.

I don't bother leashing Lupus because we're the only campers on site. In fact, the place is so empty and silent this early in the morning, it's eerie, like he and I are the last living creatures on a post-nuclear winter Earth. Snow drifts down in wind-buffeted fragments from the still leafy trees. No dog barks, no human voice calls out. Then, no sooner do I acknowledge the strange silence than two squirrels begin chattering at one another in a nearby tree. Reality returns.

The sun shines silently, the wind sleeps. Something, a voice in my head, begins to suggest that maybe we should stay here despite winter's prematurity. But this temptation is just my characteristic ambivalence asserting itself, a brief, fickle change of heart about returning to Ontario, a trepidation in knowing that two days from now I will have to testify that my important dream of a new beginning out west didn't work out the way I wanted it to. My fancy retreats to the place I am determined that it belongs, behind the door of a closet in a dank room forgotten inside the recesses of my mind.

I make coffee, letting it perk while I roll up my sleeping bag. I take down the tent and pack the trunk. It's early and, passing the campground facilities as we drive out, I decide to take a shower, a luxury that will be denied me the rest of my journey back. Agreeably, Lupus waits for me in the car, assuming that because I leave him there I am not going to depart without him. Lupus, as far as I know, has only one fear: being abandoned by his best friend.

We're on the road by nine. We're in Manitoba by ten.

I telephone my partner/former partner from some dark and battle-weary village still several hours north of Thunder Bay. Calling collect, I nearly provide the operator with my full name, as though my partner will need my surname to remember who I am.

"I'm in Ontario," I say, after she accepts the charges. "I'm coming back."

She expresses no surprise.

"I came second at that job in Drumheller," I explain.

"When will you get in?" she asks.

"Tomorrow night, late. I haven't made Thunder Bay yet. I've another thousand miles to drive after Thunder Bay."

"How's Lupus?"

"He's fine."

"I'll wait up," she says.

"It could be really late."

"I'll wait up."

Staying up late at times is how *she* approaches freedom. Up at night, asleep during the day, all depending on her daily whim. This kind of independence doesn't demand much, and you don't have to commit yourself to it very deeply. Maybe

I should learn from her to assert myself this way. Except it doesn't seem like enough to me. Her brand of independence is like crossing against the light or spitting on the sidewalk, then calling yourself a rebel.

As I drive deeper into my second night on the road, I think about her and me and our gradual dissolution at her hands. She's been pushing me away. I've heard it in her voice over the two months I've been out west. The last time I called her was from the telephone in my brother's office. I told her I'd been interviewed for a radio job in the Alberta badlands and would know in a couple of days if I was hired or not.

"Is that what you want?" she asked.

"I don't have any choice," I said. "I have to get a job."

She said nothing. There was a deep chill in her voice that day.

"What's wrong?" I said. "Every time I call, you seem further away. You don't want to come out west, do you?"

"I have children here."

"But they're all grown up."

Silence.

I sighed.

She said nothing.

We terminated the conversation shortly thereafter, accomplishing even less in this call than in the several phone calls preceding it.

There are things she's not telling me. I can hear their absence. They are like disconsolate fans leaving a stadium before the game is over because the game is already lost.

It's one a.m. by the time Lupus and I hit the highway that circumnavigates the city of Thunder Bay. I'm fuzzy and exhausted; we've been driving more than fifteen hours. In my fatigue, the darkness seems as thick as glue. My headlights pierce it brazenly, but it closes up as soon as we pass, falling into viscous place behind us.

I find a picnic area where I can pull in and rest. Lupus gets out and we do our business, both of us stumbling to a place at the edge of a row of trees on the verge of a dark patch of woods. We mark our territory together, then return to the car to get some sleep.

I doze sitting up behind the wheel, Lupus sleeps on the passenger seat. When morning comes, I am surprised by the intensity of the dawn, by how completely it has replaced my deep recollection of the previous night.

We drive. I think of how fragile Lupus and I are in our present circumstances. I have no extra money. If the car breaks down, even if a tire goes flat, no matter where we happen to be, that will become the place where we must live and work, at least until we can afford to repair the damage. I toy with the notion of disaster. One half of me is afraid of the prospect, the other delights in it.

I stop the car to make coffee, the Coleman stove perched on the gravel shoulder of the highway. Lupus won't eat or drink. When we depart, we're like shell-shocked soldiers stumbling along Ontario's highways in a clumsy daze. Morning gives way to afternoon, afternoon to evening. At last, I eat the dregs of the food I prepared the night before we departed Calgary, sandwiches in plastic wrap, the last of the food we have. It's still cold outside, but gradually warming up as we head east. I don't have the heart to play any music as I drive: I'm going the wrong way, back to Ontario, and I'd rather retreat in silence.

The temperature rises more quickly as we head south. After dark it begins to rain. I keep buying gasoline and counting the diminishing pile of twenties in my threadbare wallet. I make my last gasoline purchase at one a.m. I have a dollar and fifteen cents left and cannot fill the tank. It's going to be close. The downpour is so relentless it seems almost biblical. *Noah, the ark, how big is a cubit?* I touch the right front pocket of my jeans with my fingertips, making sure I still have the dollar-fifteen, my tiny emergency fund.

The fuel light hiccups on just after we reach Highway 401. It's beyond the middle of the night, and Lupus and I are alone on the hissing asphalt except for the rampaging tractor-trailers that charge through the darkness and the rain like Christmas-lighted dragons. At first, the fuel light can't decide whether to stay on. It blinks off a couple of times before remaining on at last. I glance at it frequently, imagining that it gets brighter with each passing moment, growing shriller and shriller in its warning the longer I seem to ignore it. I've been in this position before, only a few weeks ago. But it was daylight then. The fuel light didn't shriek that time the way it does now in the darkness.

It won't stop raining. It's been raining all night long. Some great, foolish sense of self-importance convinces me it's raining the whole world over.

We make it to Kingston, though, fuel light on and all. We reach the familiar city, then the street that history has relegated to the wrong side of the tracks. Eventually I locate the rundown apartment building that my partner of more than six years preferred to accompanying me out west. I recall Bob Seger's song "You'll Accomp'ny Me."

I turn off the ignition and the fuel light at last goes out.

Lupus gets up beside me. He glances at me inquiringly as I sit holding the steering wheel for a long moment or two, on the cusp of a decision, perhaps, but too exhausted to follow through. I don't know what I'm doing here. I don't know what I'm doing anywhere.

I would sit here longer, except for Lupus, who glances at me every few seconds. So I sigh and remove the keys from the steering column, forcing them into the same pocket that holds my last dollar and fifteen cents. Then I reach down in the darkness and find the pool of metal that is his leash. I connect it to the chain around his neck, and we dart into the downpour of the cold, vindictive rain. The wind seems forlorn, disconsolate, and I realize almost instantly that the relationship I left behind when I went out west has come to an end. But I don't want to admit it yet.

It's nearly five a.m., and I've been driving almost twenty-four hours straight. I carry my physical exhaustion like a suit of armour. It protects me, my exhaustion, from everything that happens after I gently knock on my partner's door.

We embrace, me more tightly than her. We drink coffee, although I don't register its taste. I drink as if in a trance, absently running my fingers across the mug, which was purchased at some happier time in our shared past. We mostly talk about Lupus and the drive from Calgary, topics that don't matter as much as what is left unsaid. Lupus finds a spot in a nearby corner, curls up, dozes. My partner/former partner suggests that I retrieve my sleeping bag and set it up on her living room floor. I know this is a significant suggestion, that she's prepared it in advance, but it's dawn and I'm too tired to make an issue of it. I'll deal with all of the implications of her not allowing me into her bed once I've managed to get some sleep. But I can see she's been preparing to tell me our relationship is over, to shake her head in sad superiority because I haven't already figured this out myself.

I sleep until noon, fitfully but densely. After I wake, we have coffee again. I suppose something in me wants to convey that I haven't been away very long, that little, if anything, has changed for me during my absence. I nearly tell her I shouldn't have gone in the first place, surrendering, I suppose, to that familiar urge that makes a man plead guilty to various crimes he didn't commit. Or is it just that I still think I can manipulate my life and the people I want to be in it by becoming the kind of person they would prefer me to be?

"Shall I make dinner tonight?" I ask her. "Do you have any food?"

But she doesn't answer me. She simply gets up and walks off down the hall towards the bedroom.

She has never cooked during our years together. I did all the cooking, for her, for some of her children. Hers was an honest militancy: at the end of her first marriage she said she'd never cook again, and I didn't begrudge her this. I enjoy cooking, so I didn't mind.

"Shall I make dinner tonight?" I ask again when she returns.

"No. I don't want that," she snaps.

"I don't mind," I persist.

When she glares at me, I understand her problem. A meal would represent some vague restaking of claim. I must accept that I am now intruding on the world she created for herself while I was away.

"You can't stay here," she says. "It's my place. You have to find your own."

I am silent a long time after this. I feel betrayed. I suppose I could dig with a shovel at the rubble of unanswered questions until I unearthed the truth, but I don't have the strength to make the effort.

"I see," I say at last.

She knows someone, she explains, who is looking for a boarder.

"And Lupus?"

"Lupus wouldn't be happy here. Besides," she tells me, "you and Lupus are peas in a pod, whether *you* know it or not."

And so I find a place for Lupus and me somewhere else in the city. Despite his insistence on my sweeping the stairs and cleaning the shower, my landlord and I try at first to become friends. We recognize a common bond in our respective desires to authenticate ourselves by gaining social acceptance, and together we make efforts to pursue this elusive goal. We do so by looking for work, by sometimes finding it, by foolishly believing it will last. We do so by stepping out into the glare of the city's nightlife, trying to find an identity for ourselves by getting lost in a crowd.

My landlord is fond of a karaoke bar near the waterfront. We approach these outings differently. He sings at the microphone—"Born To Be Wild," in a powerful baritone—while I linger in the audience wondering why we're here. He buys women drinks with money he cannot afford, while I nurse a drink or two by myself, eventually switching to coffee. Sometimes he's miffed that I am so reserved, but my only desire is to blend with the void and stay close to the exit. I sit at the bar, feeling sorry for us, because we're aging and visibly lonely, and because we can't seem to break away from this loneliness. Now and then I glance at a woman sitting across the bar, and she glances at me. Not a meaningful connection, it only lasts a moment or two. I think the moment reflects nothing more than a shrug of mutual embarrassment.

Lupus doesn't like these few nights when I leave him at home alone. I imagine he disapproves of where I've been and how pointless my being there was; when he pisses on my bed, I forgive him because part of me suspects that he might be right.

My former partner calls to suggest that I pick up my things from her apartment. I do this gratefully, although I discover in the process that she's sold some of them or given them to her kids. But I take my stereo, my television, my VCR, my bed, a couple of dressers. I'm glad to bring them home with me, especially the bed. Since my return from Alberta, I've been sleeping on the floor, using the mattresses and the sleeping bag I took out west with me. I haven't slept in a conventional bed for four months.

We stay in touch, but uneasily. I can't tell which one of us is resisting letting go. Sometimes I think it's her, sometimes I think it could be me. We seem to drift back and forth between giving up and giving in, with Lupus as some patient observer of the growing wasteland between us. I can't help but suspect that he knows how things will end, whether he likes it or not.

A couple of days before my birthday, near the end of November, my former partner visits with a card and a coffee mug. The mug has Sagittarius depicted on its sides in colourful illustration. She's a Sagittarian, too, and neither one of us has ever determined whether this is good or bad, or whether it matters much at all. Still, I notice that she gives me a mug I could just as easily have given her. Perhaps the problem is we're too much the same.

On my actual birthday, she tells me she's begun seeing someone else.

"You met him once," she says. "He's from El Salvador."

About a month later she calls to tell me that she and her new man are going back to his native country. Her tone when she tells me this is one of unexpected anger, like I've driven her to this. She tells me that she needs some time away, that our six years together wore her out. I have an extraordinary energy, she contends, and it was hard for her to keep up. "Six years with you is like thirty with a normal person," she says. "In the end I realized I was just exhausted."

"What about your kids?" I say.

"They're old enough to fend for themselves," she replies. "That's what they tell me, anyway."

In the ensuing silence, I soak in the realization she used her children as an excuse for not going out west with me. I say nothing, though. Not mentioning it is a matter of dignity.

Thinking about this later, I feel some anger of my own. More at myself than her. I recall the time, more than five years before, when I first asked her to move out west with me. She initially said yes, wanting to be with me. But then she changed her mind. She wanted to remain where we were. I suffered for three days over her change of heart, trying to figure out whether I should simply go myself. But I was in love at the time. I transformed my caring into obligation, convincing myself that doing so was noble. So I stayed with her and her children, and started the newspaper instead. We were obligated to each other: I was obliged to feed and house us, she was obliged to help me with the newspaper.

Now, looking back in angry hindsight, I wish I'd left back then. Had I done so, I might have found an identity for myself that I was more comfortable with. Certainly I would have avoided the newspaper project that ultimately almost killed me. Ironic, really, that I decided to stay back then, in view of her decision to go to El Salvador now. Irony's okay when you glimpse it from afar, but up close it is something else. It can stimulate deep regret.

In January I receive my first letter from El Salvador. It's one of those confessional letters people shouldn't write. In matters of the heart, ignorance is a special kind of bliss. Her letter tells me about things she did in her panic while I was out west. Love affairs. Her feelings of abandonment because I had gone away. I must read her words of remorseful suffering, her confession of revenge, with a suffering of my own. Whether this suffering arises out of love or vanity I can't determine now. I only know I feel betrayed and hurt.

But I write her back the very next day, forgiving her for everything. My landlord argues that to forgive in this way is the hallmark of a fool. "I can't forgive a woman who breaks my heart," he insists defiantly, his hands formed into fists.

I ponder his words for a moment before I answer him. "It's *my* heart," I counter at last. "*I'm* the one with the power to break it or not." And hearing what I've said, I hope that it's true.

As for Lupus? Although he misses my former partner, his heart is unbroken, too. There's too much life to live for him to allow himself to be laid low by just one loss. Life is supposed to be rich, I decide, because it isn't supposed to be long. Lupus already knows this.

One day the following spring as we stroll out of the racetrack, Lupus suddenly dashes across the street to greet a tall woman walking along the sidewalk on the other side of the road. I race after him, his leash draped around my neck, calling him back to me, afraid the woman will be frightened.

I apologize to her as I connect him to his leash.

"That's okay," she says with a smile, gazing at Lupus and remarking what a handsome fellow he is.

She's soon gone and, by this time, Lupus wants to get on with his walk.

It wasn't our former partner, and it never can be. Lupus and I go on.

August 1993

"I guess there's something I should confess," my travelling companion tells me on the morning we finally part company in the middle of British Columbia.

"What's that?" I ask.

"I don't like driving and I don't like camping," he replies, not sheepish in the least about his announcement.

I gaze at him a moment, hardly surprised by the news, but nonplussed that he would feel compelled to admit it now that it's too late. "Now you tell me," I say, not so much to him but in the general direction of adversarial fate.

We stand at the edge of our vacant campsite, glancing uneasily at one another, perhaps deciding whether or not to embark on some kind of quarrel. But shortly we give up, smiling and shaking our heads in wistful resignation instead. What difference does it make now? I conclude. He's here at his destination. Is it his fault that mine — so vague and premature — eludes me still?

We've been travelling together, two cars in convoy, for exactly four weeks, ever since that hot and humid day at the end of July when we departed eastern Ontario. Since then I've felt like a babysitter, by turns annoyed and guilty because he turned out to be so satisfied to have someone to watch over him. Now, on this fine and sunny late August morning, we have broken camp together for the last time. He will drive a few miles into Kelowna to stay with relatives until he finds his own place to live. Lupus and I intend to travel deeper into British Columbia, losing ourselves more completely in the mountains, in our continued pursuit of the spiritual destination I commenced seeking four weeks ago.

Where this quest is concerned, I blame myself for not having found what I'm looking for. I suspect that it is me, not the odyssey itself, that has failed. New beginnings require letting go of past obligations and rituals. So far I haven't let go of nearly enough. It occurs to me that I might be trying too hard.

For the most part, I try not to think about the spiritual epiphany that eludes me, or why it seems so illusory. I stare instead out across Lake Okanagan, admiring the way the morning sunshine sparkles on its ripples.

"No rattlesnakes in your tent," I remind my companion at last.

"Thank goodness for *that,*" he remarks.

This rattlesnake business has been a running joke between

us, and my companion grins good-naturedly. For four weeks, he's dutifully read the lists of hazards posted on the bulletin board in each provincial park at which we stop, returning to our campsite afterwards to relate them to me. Poison ivy, most of the time, though sometimes bears or other large animals reputably linger on the outskirts of certain provincial campgrounds, a reminder of the wilderness on which we humans are intruding. Here, in the Okanagan Valley, he discovered rattlesnakes at the bottom of the list. When he reported this to me his expression was solemn and perplexed. He fretted about what might slither under his tent, the venomous fangs that could penetrate the plastic floor of the tent and the down of his sleeping bag, eventually piercing his delicate flesh.

"What time are your relatives expecting you?" I ask him.

"Any time before twelve. I didn't know how long it'd take to pack our gear. God, I'm looking forward to sleeping in a bed."

I simply shrug. Contemplating a turning point in my life, I've come to believe that where I sleep doesn't matter much.

We linger by our cars a few moments longer, paying tribute, I suppose, to four weeks of travel and an association that has now grown hazy in the miles that have disappeared behind us. I remain dismayed that my flirtations with the kind of adventure I hoped would immerse me more completely on this trip have been astonishingly brief. So I've been looking forward to the day when Lupus and I are finally able to go on alone. But this parting is a week later than expected and I'm deeply disappointed. The delay in reaching Kelowna has cost me dearly, in just about every way. My resources, energy, and means are seriously depleted.

—

My companion is sixty-five. We've been friends for more than three years. I first met him in a restaurant not far from where I operated my newspaper. As we regularly encountered each other over hurried, desperate dinners, we progressed from fragile nods and greetings to longer conversations, and we eventually began taking our meals together. When he told me that he wanted a job to supplement his pension income, I hired him to work with us at the newspaper, more or less as a receptionist. He was a widower, and the job gave him something to do, earned him a little extra money, and provided him with an additional excuse to escape his empty apartment.

It's hard to say who adopted whom. But we became close friends, almost like family; the relationship felt so natural and unassuming. To Lupus, too. He would hurry to the window whenever he heard my friend's car pull up our long driveway. Even after the newspaper's last gasp, all of us — my partner, my friend, Lupus, and I — gathered three or four times a week to bolster each other's spirits. For Lupus, I think this was a bridge between the weeks he'd spent lying patiently in the newspaper office while we humans toiled away and the worrisome period afterwards when none of us had anywhere to go.

Strange, though, since the moment we left Ontario, Lupus has tended to ignore my travelling companion. On the road, he's been attached, more exclusively, to me. Sometimes I even speculate that he shares my sense of disappointment and failure. The original idea was for Lupus and I to go out west on our own. Then, this past spring, to my surprise the trip evolved into a joint venture between me and my companion. In the end, my plan was co-opted by *his* plan. My plan was for Lupus and I to camp our way out west. I would find a new place to live and work in the mountains and my romantic partner would join us once we were settled. His plan? Originally he planned to ship his things to Kelowna, there being little to keep him in Ontario now that his wife and the newspaper were both dead and hopelessly gone. He would follow his belongings by train or by air, and later, when Lupus and I arrived out west, I was to look him up.

But one evening that spring, scant moments after enjoying dinner with us, he suddenly toppled from his place at our table, crashing to our kitchen floor. Cardiac arrest. I called an ambulance while my partner pounded on his chest, shrieking his name loudly to summon him back. Miraculously, he lived. In the hostpital they put in a pacemaker. In the hospital, some of his friends decided that perhaps it would be best, because he remained intent on moving west, that he tag along with me so that I could keep an eye on him.

I concurred that their plan was appropriate under the circumstances. Feeling responsible, and believing I had found additional purpose by this new, unexpected obligation, I prepared the route we would take, sacrificing the spontaneity I had intended to employ while travelling on my own with Lupus. I calculated that taking three weeks to arrive in Kelowna represented a leisurely pace that would put little strain on him. Once there, Lupus and I would go on alone, our mission accomplished.

Going on was integral to *my* plan. I wanted to camp with Lupus at Pacific Rim on the far shore of Vancouver Island. I imagined Lupus and I standing there with our toes in the

Pacific Ocean, both of us empowered by a new and limitless horizon. As I imagined Lupus and myself at the edge of the Pacific Ocean, I fancied buying an Aleutian island, my partner would come west and join us, and she, Lupus and I would live together on the island where no one would ever find us. I imagined us disappearing into some void. I would escape everything I'd done wrong in the past and wash away my sins in some mystical river. Then I would be a different man — cured, healed, changed. We could live our lives more honestly, I imagined, with breathless enthusiasm, in simple clarity, in primitive freedom. How much I wanted then, how vast and pleasantly — even wonderfully — ill-defined my imagination was. I was forty-four years old. Who knew how much time remained for me? I could no longer accept wasting any of my life.

But as we made our way across Canada's vast landmass, filling us with awe at its deep wilderness and expansive prairie, three weeks turned into four. I soon discovered that my leisurely three-week time frame was not leisurely enough for my companion. I'd planned for us to stay in some parks for only one day. I'd wanted to alternate, one night, then two. In the end, though, it was rare that we camped in the same location for only a single night. Before I knew it, an extra week had escaped my grasp.

Now I stand here on the shores of Lake Okanagan with only a few hundred dollars left. My share of the additional campsite fees and the extra food have taken a serious toll on my finances. I have determined that I won't be able to afford the ferry from the mainland to Vancouver Island now. Lupus and I have no hope of reaching Pacific Rim. So I stand here with my friend, feeling naked, even desperate. I intend to go on, I *must* go on, but this intense compulsion is compromised by a feeling of nagging hopelessness. How far Lupus and I get, how long we can look after ourselves, will depend upon how frugal I can be.

It's obvious I've been defeated yet again by too much obligation. While I've helped someone else achieve his goal, my own is little more than a mirage shimmering in the distance.

At the edge of our empty campsite I remove Lupus's leash and open the car door for him. Anxious to be going, he hops onto the front seat. I close the door behind him and he sticks his head out the window, watching his human associates embark on a ceremonial farewell that makes no sense to him, that he may even suspect contains a measure of artificiality.

"Well, compadre," I say.

My companion and I embrace.

"When you come back to Kelowna, call me, and I'll put you two up until you find your feet," he says.

I thank him for his invitation. I do appreciate it. Yet returning to Kelowna, I believe, would feel like some kind of defeat. Kelowna was his destination, not mine. I lived there many years ago and didn't like it much, so I soon moved on. Since I left, those aspects of Kelowna that I fled from — its conservatism, materialism, and complacency — have become even more pronounced. I have no intention of living here again. It would be like signing on for a mission with an objective I don't respect.

We climb into our cars and drive out of the provincial park. On the highway a few moments later, my companion turns east towards his destination. Lupus and I head west. We wave at one another clumsily as we part.

I will talk to him on the telephone a couple of times before he dies in his living room chair in less than a year.

Later that day, my brief sense of feeling free and unburdened grows fragile. At the edge of celebration I remain preoccupied by various fears and worries. How far can Lupus and I go with so little money remaining? When I phone home to Ontario tell my partner that Lupus and I are safe, to convince her yet again that she'll love it out here with us, why does the phone ring ten times without her picking it up? Has the woman I've left behind already moved on without me? Have I been foolish to assume that everything I did before I left Ontario mattered in any way, that my excessive labours helped the world turn more purposefully, that my efforts gave me value and acceptance?

We camp that afternoon in Manning Provincial Park. I book our site for three nights because I have decided Lupus and I need to regroup, to truly understand that we are at last on our own. I want to sit at our campsite picnic table and write in the sunshine for three days. I haven't been able to write for weeks, because I was busy handling the long list of demands my travelling arrangements foisted on me. Now I just want to put something down on paper. I don't care much what is it is. Something, anything, that denotes that I have begun, that *we* have begun, Lupus and I, that there's a new life for us out here and we are hunting it down like prey to feed our spiritual hunger, to prevent our spiritual starvation. It's a corny axiom, I know, but at this moment I truly want this pleasant summer's day to be the first day of the rest of my life.

Later that afternoon a man identifying himself as a park biologist, tall, grizzled, and rugged, wanders into our site. "I heard about your dog," he says. "I wanted to see him for myself."

"Lupus?"

"Lupus," he repeats, nodding appreciatively. "That's a good name for him."

Lupus has been dozing not far away at his end of a long chain tied to the picnic table. He's not a good watchdog; he's too aloof for the job, and he has not moved since this stranger joined us here. But now, hearing his name, he grows curious and approaches our visitor cautiously.

I introduce him.

"What do you think you have here?" the biologist asks me, studying Lupus critically.

"A Siberian husky," I reply. "But I'm told there's wolf in there."

"Well," says the biologist with that rustic certainty one encounters frequently in people used to the wilderness, "what you have here is a wolf with some Siberian husky or maybe German shepherd."

I gape at him. I'm surprised, yet not surprised. Perhaps I've always suspected Lupus was more wolf than dog, but until now I have only been speculating.

"Let me show you," our visitor says.

He goes over Lupus thoroughly, taking me on a guided tour

of the distinctions defining what is wolf and what is dog. He examines and discusses his tail, ears, chest, feet, teeth, and a variety of other parts in a detailed, informative lecture.

"Siberians are stockier. This guy's thin, with a narrow chest, built for speed. Husky height, though. Husky ears. Wolf teeth." The biologist regains his height and Lupus slips away to lie down again. "This guy's more wolf than dog. It's there if you know your wolves. I'll bet he can fly."

I nod. "And you can't hear him coming."

"Just like a ghost, right?"

"Funny you should mention that. I wanted to call him Ghost after I got to know him better, but it was too late. By then he was Lupus. He answered to that name right away."

We stand there a moment in silence, both of us gazing down at him.

"I guess you've explained a lot," I say with a shrug. "To tell you the truth, he doesn't act like any dog I've ever had."

The biologist is surprised to learn that I retrieved Lupus from the pound. "How'd he end up there?" he wants to know.

I tell him I'm not sure.

"Well, he seems friendly enough."

"Oh, yeah," I respond. "In a snooty sort of way."

"Does he ever get aggressive?"

"No."

"You're a lucky man, you know."

I glance at Lupus who is watching us, his handsome face framed between his paws. "Yeah, I know," I say.

An interpretive officer with the park also comes to see Lupus that day, an hour or so later, while we are having dinner. She tells me she is giving a talk that evening in the outdoor theatre not far from where we're camped. She's going to discuss the various dogs and cats that live in the park: wolves and foxes, cougars and lynx. She'd like it very much if I brought Lupus along. I promise her I will.

At the young woman's presentation I take an aisle seat and Lupus lies down beside me. Midway through her program she introduces him to the various campers there. Lupus, being very much a ham and knowing he has everyone's attention, rises to the occasion. Unasked, he delivers a series of howls to amuse his admiring audience. The crowd responds with laugher and applause.

By the end of the program, however, he has become too stimulated by all the attention. He sits up on a seat beside me and tries to wrestle with me. As people gather around to meet him, he shows off shamelessly. He becomes rough. When he won't behave himself, I must take him by the ruff and ferociously growl at him. Most who have gathered around us are amused by this method. But it works: Lupus gradually settles down.

"He thinks he should be in the movies," I remark with some embarrassment just before we all disperse.

"*White Fang 2* or *3*," someone quips.

"Something like that," I reply.

"He knows he's a striking fellow."

"Unfortunately, he does."

It rains most of the next day. We are camped well up in the mountains and the temperature drops rapidly. I hate the rain.

Lupus and I have nothing to do. Beyond brief walks in the drizzle, we spend much of the day in our small tent or sitting in the car, my clothing damp, our breath a fog in front of our faces. We listen to the rain rattle on the roof of our tent or watch it bead on the car windshield like counterfeit pieces of silver. I make lunch in the rain, climb back into the tent. Later we sit in the car again.

I try to write in the tent, lying on my belly, then turning onto my back and propping my scribbler against my knees. Nothing happens. In the car, the steering wheel is in the way. I try to convince Lupus to change places with me, but he'll sit behind the wheel only when he wants to and not otherwise.

On Saturday I try several times to telephone my partner back in Ontario from a phone booth five miles down the mountain, scheduling these calls in strict two-hour intervals, inadvertently making a wasteland of the valuable time in between. She does not answer any of my calls. The day drags by, then the night. I read until dark, then lie in the tent like a caged animal, Lupus dozing beside me. He has been more accepting of this wasted day than I have, more resigned to it. I feel imprisoned by it. My higher expectations lead to deeper disappointment, I suppose. But what's the alternative? Lower my expectations? I've already lived too much of my life shrinking my options and modifying my needs to reflect those of the world around me.

I try to think about the freedom I now enjoy, to put a worthwhile spin on my current situation as a way of divining some sort of solace from it. But I am unable to do this. I feel merely worried and trapped, preoccupied by doubt. Each thought is like a skip in an old, worn record, playing itself in a rude hiccup over and over in my mind.

The next day it rains again. I grow more hopeless and desperate. I drive down the mountain to the telephone booth six times to listen to the unanswered rings of my partner's telephone. I hate myself for my desperation, but I make the calls anyway. There's something so familiar about this kind of self-inflicted torture. Something about it seems so easy.

On Monday Lupus and I must leave. The sun comes out, and the temperature rises. We break camp after I have coffee, then drive down the mountain to the highway, looking for a service station. We turn left and head towards an intersection with the Trans-Canada Highway a few miles away. There Lupus and I will make a decision: west to the coast or east towards Kelowna. Ahead or backwards. Embracing our faint hope or turning away from it and surrendering to disappointment. After I buy gasoline, I count our money. I have barely a hundred dollars left. We have three days' worth of food. Camping, we can afford three or four nights in fees. After that? I just don't know.

I feel both exhilaration and despair at once. I can almost hear them arguing in my mind, a debate that grows more and more shrill. Each side tries to shout down the other. Neither of these personal, psychological politicians can be trusted. They're just vying for a majority. Is it good to be afraid and stupid to be careless? Or is it the reverse? The questions seem endless. I do not govern myself; I am governed only by the repeated questions and the apparent futility of the debate.

In the end, I leave the decision over which way we'll go entirely up to Lupus. As we wait at a stop sign for the traffic on the Trans-Canada to clear, I ask him in which direction we should turn. He sits up on the seat beside me. He glances at me a moment. I wait, watching him for a sign. Then, eventually, ever so slightly, he tilts his head to the left.

"Vancouver," I say. "Are you sure?"

But he has already spoken. I don't expect further response. Feeling newly released from the responsibility of caution, I turn west towards the coast. I'm aware that Lupus's gesture was really nothing more than a coin toss, but his choice seems more credible than mine.

We take the ferry—not the one to Vancouver Island, but one that will cruise a few miles along the shoreline on its way to the Sunshine Coast. This we can afford. We may not be headed for Pacific Rim, but at least we're going forward instead of returning the way we've come.

Signs shriek from various pillars in the bowels of the boat, telling us that dogs are not allowed on the upper decks. I must leave Lupus in the car, the windows partially down. When I glance back at him, so out of place in this forest of vehicles, more gas escapes from my deflating balloon of hope. Lupus and I are so close now, I share his disappointments empathetically.

I remain on the deck with my peers for only a few minutes. I feel like a stranger among them, standing at the windows to admire the passing seascape. They read newspapers or nibble on chocolate bars. I am a vagrant. I cling to the long skirt of their society like a toddler, its folds clenched in my tiny fists as I try desperately to hang on.

I return to the car to sit with Lupus. He does not wag his

tail but simply lies down on the passenger seat, apparently not surprised that I have returned.

"Just you and me, Loop," I say.

He curls up. He knows. Someday, I imagine him thinking, you'll rid yourself of this habit of stating the obvious.

Gibson's Landing displays an odd assortment of signs and facades in various downtown locations, the meaning of which I'm unable to puzzle out. I soon discover that the community is pretending to be Castle Rock, Maine. They're shooting a movie here, Stephen King's *Needful Things.* Fictional storefronts peer down on the street, flimsily attached by bolts to the reality they temporarily replace. Poles on the fronts of some of the buildings jut out and upwards in that lusty, familiar angle that reminds me of an urgent phallus, American flags dangling from their ends. Siddhartha meets Rome meets the United States of America. The place is as confused about its identity as I am about mine.

We manage to find our way out of this strangely conflicted town, and we continue down the highway to Sechelt, then on to another provincial park not far away. I pitch our tent and make lunch. It's still a beautiful day, warm and sunny. I'm glad. I enjoy the outdoors here, and I'd like a few days without rain. Passing through Sechelt, I made a mental note to check out job opportunities here. Maybe this is *the place,* I decide impulsively. Maybe when I telephone Ontario today my partner will answer. When she does, I'll have something more enticing to sell her: a place, a job, a plan, something that will measure and define my worth. I still believe that I must achieve these things to earn somebody's love.

I count my money and decide that I can afford to stay in the park for two nights. Tomorrow I'll see what I can do about finding work.

The rest of the day is peaceful, and I even manage to write for a couple of hours. I resist the urge to walk to the pay phone near the park entrance to call my partner. Tomorrow will be soon enough; by then I hope to have something encouraging to report.

A couple in their early forties camps in the site next to me. They are newly in love, but they take time out from their romantic euphoria to admire Lupus. I envy them the relentless intensity their passion still contains. They have not yet settled into the more mundane routine that begins to creep into a relationship over time. I wonder whether there is anything that lovers can do to minimize the usual ritualized impediments to lasting love.

Lupus and I sit at a campfire that evening. He lies out of range of the flames; I must reach back into the darkness to touch him. It's such a peaceful night, pleasantly reflective. I feel renewed hope. Alone like this, I think I can discover the tranquility my inner voice tells me I am seeking. I feel because I am. I am because I feel. I am a Descartes of the heart, I suppose. I *do* think, but it's a more difficult process for me, trapped as I am in societal regulations that are so limited and narrow, so self-serving and unimaginative. What we feel, I believe, makes us unique. Too often our thoughts are framed not by our feelings or our instincts but by what we believe we *should* think.

There's no work in Sechelt, I discover. None. I visit the employment centre, and there are no jobs posted. I peruse the community newspapers and turn up only one editor's job at the newspaper in Gibson's. But this discovery puts me into a quandary. I have twenty years experience as a newspaperman, but the newspaper I owned until just a few months ago nearly snapped me like a wooden match. Newspaper work is a demanding occupation in its own right, never mind if you've already burned yourself out through years of newsrooms and meetings, then seen a newspaper of your own, which you built from the ground up, collapse around you. I know my doctor back in Ontario would prefer I stay away from the newspaper business for now. But I equivocate. Maybe tomorrow, when my depleted financial resources force me to make a decision again, maybe that's when I should contemplate returning to an occupation in which I run the risk of doing serious harm to my mental and physical stability.

Before I even contemplate going back to newspaper work, though, I want to make sure I explore all the other options. There's a college campus here, a satellite of the main campus in Vancouver. My partner is a teacher who can't find a teaching job in Ontario. Perhaps here there's a possibility, for her as well as for me. She could find a posting here in their English department. Something else I can use to sell this place to her when she finally answers her telephone.

That evening, when I dial my partner's number the phone still goes unanswered. Is she all right? I wonder. I hang up the phone and return with Lupus to our campsite to build another fire. I try to recapture the serenity I achieved the previous night, the tranquility I found in the warm flames and the starlit sky, in my friendship with Lupus. But I can't. Quiet panic has set in. I become preoccupied again with the prospect of running out of time and funds.

I begin the next day by sorting through goals and strategies, then handwriting a resumé outlining my experience and what I've been trained to term "achievements." I feel responsible now, focused by a sense of obligation that drives me to get going, to try to recover the safety I hope resides in respectability.

I decide to go back to what is familiar; there is no time to contemplate any other option. I telephone the publisher and I sit outside the newspaper offices, at a picnic table where some of the staff eat lunch, where she will speak with me. Although she has an opening for an editor, she already has someone in mind for the position. Her newspaper is part of a chain, there's movement back and forth among the employees at the various papers. She confesses that the publishers enjoy stealing one another's editorial staff.

Still, she thinks there might be an opening at the newspaper in Squamish. Would I consider an interview with the publisher there? I tell her that I would. She makes the appropriate telephone call.

When she returns, she catches me checking my wallet. I don't have much money left, I admit, and she lends me twenty dollars to make sure I can go on. It's a kind and understanding loan.

I am gratified when, a couple of months down the road, I am able to repay her. By that point I am back in Ontario. I feel the need to explain to her why I had to leave British Columbia. I tell her that I failed to achieve what I hoped for in British Columbia. I do not tell her how or why.

Lupus and I take the ferry back to Vancouver, then turn north, driving the Sea to Sky Highway, headed for Squamish.

When we arrive there, the results are much the same. There is an opening, but . . .

"You published your own newspaper, I see here," the publisher says, glancing at my handwritten resumé.

"Yes."

"You have more experience that I do," she notes, fixing me with a stare.

I am politely silent. I resort to a shrug.

"You could end up doing *my* job."

I don't *want* her job. But telling her this will achieve nothing. I know the interview is all but over. We sit there in awkward silence.

She sighs. "You should probably talk to the company vice-president. Do you want me to call him?"

"That's very kind of you," I say, an obsequious mask glued to the flesh of my face.

The vice-president is in Whistler, some distance up the coast. I am to see him the following morning. Lupus and I drive further north, while the afternoon wanes in jagged fragments between the breathtaking mountain peaks around us.

"I don't know, Loop," I say, wanting to hear myself admit it. And I *don't* know.

We find a place just outside of Whistler in a tiny but pleasant park called Brandy Wine. There's no one else here for the moment, and I let Lupus have a run. Outside of our daily walks, he's had little exercise in the days since we began our journey. He streaks in exuberant circles around a field in the middle of the park, joyful and excited. He goes all out, leaping various obstacles, dashing here and there in sharp, imaginative angles, returning when I call him, but only to dart by my knees as closely as he can, obliquely bringing me into the game and the ecstasy of his release.

Watching him run this way, I am overwhelmed by deep emotion. My eyes suddenly well up with tears. I feel my ambivalence and confusion begin to ebb away like the soreness in shoulder muscles after a heavy pack is finally lowered to the ground. I begin to see the foolishness behind riding this long train of interviews for newspaper jobs. I'm not ready yet; it hasn't been long enough since my physical collapse. My job hunt has been motivated negatively, I decide, by the terror of uncertainty. This is unfamiliar territory for me. I'm afraid of indefinition, of solitude.

Lupus dashes by again, and I grin. Witnessing his enthusiasm and spirit, everything seems possible to me.

"Atta boy, Loop," I say when at last he turns to stand beside my leg, panting from his exertions. I pet him on the shoulder in love and gratitude.

That night, despite relentless feelings of irresponsibility, I make up my mind to skip the interview the next morning. The decision is easier after I call my partner in Ontario and, to my surprise, she answers the phone. Instead of encouraging me to pursue gainful employment, she questions my newfound enthusiasm for returning to a line of work that nearly killed me a scant few months ago.

"You're still confused," she says with recognizable impatience.

I say nothing.

"So what about tomorrow?" she asks.

"Back to Kelowna. Not much money left."

I wait through more silence from the other end of the phone.

"I'll call you tomorrow night from Kelowna."

"All right."

"Where have you been?" I ask. "I've been calling you for several days."

She explains that she'd gone to visit an aunt and uncle in Ohio. I ask after their health. She doesn't want to talk about it much.

On my way back to Kelowna with Lupus the next day, I keep thinking about what she said and what she didn't say. This new distance between us feels like an unsanded surface under my bare feet, the slivers probing my flesh painfully. But I also think about Lupus, and his reckless run in the field the previous evening. I think about what it nearly showed me, what I almost recognized.

We don't make it to Kelowna until nearly eight p.m. I take a wrong turn along the way, costing me more than a hundred kilometres and a few litres of precious gasoline. When I arrive at last, I dial the number that my travelling companion gave me. One of his relatives answers and informs me that he's moved into an apartment of his own. I use another essential quarter to dial his new number. He seems pleased to hear from me. I tell him I'm glad he's found a place to live already. I tell him he sounds cheerful and content.

"What about you and Lupus?" he asks.

"We need a place to stay," I tell him.

Then he drops the bomb. "You're welcome to stay here," he says, "but there are no pets allowed. You'd have to find a kennel or something for Lupus."

Astonished, I turn and glance the few yards to the car where Lupus sits behind the wheel, watching me talk on the telephone.

"I can't do that. I don't have any money. Besides, Lupus stays with me."

"Well," he says, "I suppose we can work something out tomorrow."

"What about tonight?"

"I'm going to a play tonight," he replies. "In fact, they're here to pick me up. Give me a call tomorrow." He hangs up.

Shocked, I stand in the telephone booth a moment. I feel angry and betrayed. I contemplate calling him back; whether to give him a piece of my mind or to explain again how desperate my circumstances are, I can't say for sure. I check my funds. Nothing in my wallet. Change in my pocket: one dollar and twenty-five cents.

Someone wants to use the pay phone, a man my age in a charcoal suit. I slip outside offering a vague apology for making him wait, which he ignores.

I walk back to the car and stand at the half-open passenger-side window. I reach inside to stroke Lupus behind the ears. He gazes at me with a mixture of interest and disdain. I take a quick inventory of our circumstances. Three-quarters of a tank of gas. One dollar and twenty-five cents in cash. And we're out of food. Dusk is slipping into town like a cloak over our precarious circumstances.

After the man in the charcoal suit vacates the telephone booth, I hurry to reclaim it. I call Ontario. I feel a surprisingly deep relief when she answers.

I explain our circumstances, Lupus's and mine.

"Well, what are you going to do?"

"I don't know," I say. "I have to think of a place where we can stay for free."

She doesn't say anything, but I can feel her impatience again. It strikes me with a kind of painful incredulity that I am being a nuisance at this moment.

"My brother in Calgary is all that comes to mind," I tell her at last.

"How far is that?"

"It's getting dark. It could take most of the night."

She doesn't say anything.

"Okay," I sigh. "I'll call you from there, to let you know I made it."

"Okay," she says and hangs up.

I call my brother to tell him of my plan. But he's impatient, too.

"It's an eight-hour drive," he says.

"Worse," I confess. "I probably don't have enough gas."

"Well, what are you gonna do?"

Everyone keeps asking me this question, as though finding the right answer is a test of some kind, some measurement of my aptitude or guile.

"I'll call you when I'm just about out of gas," I suggest. "You could bring some in a can or something. Or bring some money, and I could fill up to get us the rest of the way."

He sighs. "I have to work tomorrow, you know."

"All right," I say, labouring to keep the frustration out of my voice. "If you don't hear from me, you'll know I'm going to make it, I've figured something else out. Otherwise, I'll call."

He supposes this is okay.

I return to the car, thinking about how I would behave if the circumstances were reversed.

"Just you and me, Loop," I say with a kind of proud hopelessness. This observation is becoming our song, some haunting ballad of loneliness or triumph, I'm not sure which. I suppose I enjoy its melody when I'm not despising it.

I realize I've disappointed everyone's conventional sensibilities. Now, judged and convicted, Lupus and I must suffer the punishment. An erstwhile travelling companion who lives in an apartment that doesn't allow pets, a woman who's tired of hearing from me, a brother who resists the inconvenience of dealing with a sibling who's fallen from grace. All these people have the advantage of knowing how people are supposed to behave and the penance spoiled children like me are supposed to do. People get what they deserve, everyone knows that. But when it comes to people like me, who so freely attempt to flout the conventional expectations of respectable society, my peers not only claim to know what we deserve, but why we deserve it: because we've chosen to live on the outside of the group, stubbornly refusing to fit in.

It will be some time yet before I learn to *comfortably* break some of convention's rules and restrictions. But at this moment, as I sit in the car with Lupus in Kelowna's gathering dusk, I clearly recognize the distaste I feel for some of society's conventional edicts, a distaste I'm beginning to sense I've repressed for years. Society survives on a staple diet of self-absorption and limited imagination, dishes, I believe, designed to make all of us the same as one another. You are what you eat? I suppose so. But various hungers remain at the end of many conventional lives. Maybe when we die, we die of some kind of subtle starvation. Maybe some of us starve to death because we don't learn to feed the hunger that arises out of our private quests or needs.

By the time Lupus and I reach Revelstoke, I cannot drive any longer without the fear of falling asleep at the wheel. I've been watching the gas gauge intently, and now my eyes are burning out of my head. I find a rest area along the highway and try to get some sleep, sitting up behind the wheel, my head on a pillow I prop up against the window. I doze, fidgeting frequently from a series of merciless muscle cramps and my fretful thoughts that won't let me sleep.

We're on the move again before dawn, spider-scuttling through the web of Rocky Mountain grades, passes, and bends. I don't have enough gasoline to get to Calgary; the fuel gauge is brutally honest about this. At Golden, I pull into an open self-serve in front of a small convenience store, wondering how much fuel I can purchase for one dollar and twenty-five cents.

Strangely, I feel deeply embarrassed that I must purchase such a small amount of gasoline, that a stranger is about to witness and then judge my material poverty. What will the attendant think of me as I give my car such a small transfusion of gasoline?

Then I remember the silver dollars.

There are nine in all. Christmas gifts from a favourite uncle when I was only a child. They are those large and heavy silver dollars this country used to mint. These particular coins date from the early fifties to 1960. I know they're worth more than nine dollars, although how much more I have no idea. I've never been interested in their value; I always intended to keep them for sentimental reasons and pass them on someday in my will, some tangible gift I could leave behind. I dig for them frantically, at last find them.

I get out of the car and pump nine dollars worth of gas, my earlier embarrassment giving way to a mild frustration. I decide to keep my dollar and a quarter as a tiny emergency fund. More gas if I don't make it all the way to Calgary? A chocolate bar to assuage my grumbling stomach? I don't know. Whatever emergency next comes loping over my hill.

"Well, I guess this is your lucky day," I say to the gaunt, bedraggled young man at the cash register.

He's suspicious until, with desperate neatness, I stack the nine silver dollars on his countertop.

"Is that all you have?" he asks, with a wistful shake of his head.

"That's all I have," I reply.

"Where you headed?"

"Calgary."

Thoughtfully he nods. "If you want a coffee, it's on the house. Self-serve. Right over there."

"Thanks."

I stumble in the direction he's indicated. "Can I have a larger one?" I ask, more or less over my shoulder.

"You bet," he says, without looking at me. He's preoccupied

at the cash register, putting nine dollars of his own into the drawer so that he can keep my silver dollars.

"Good luck," he says, as I move to leave the store.

"Thanks," I answer back, slipping outside.

I feel a strange sadness as I return to the car. My melancholy is delicate and confused, and I can't define its source. Something to do with the silver dollars, perhaps, but I wouldn't want to say for sure.

The sadness erupts more overtly later that sun-blasted morning as Lupus and I emerge from the mountains and begin driving into the foothills not far from Calgary. I discover that I am weeping and realize I have been crying for several minutes without being aware of it, too tired to notice perhaps, too defeated to acknowledge the physiological evidence of my collapse. It's not the silver dollars that make me cry. No, it's the way the mountains recede in the distance each time I glance into my rear-view mirror. It's the fact that I'm travelling east when I wanted to be going west. In my sadness and exhaustion, I don't feel like I'm driving to Calgary at all. No, my despair is much worse than that. I'm falling out of my personal sky. I'm going to crash in a place far south of the heaven I'd envisioned.

I weep for several minutes, still glancing intermittently in my rear-view at the mountains evaporating behind me. Eventually, I make myself get over it by touching Lupus as I drive. I pet his head, I stroke his ears as he dozes on the passenger seat, compressed into his husky curl, tolerating my need to be affectionate the way he always has. Still, regardless of his inherent reserve, I take something hopeful from him and dress my soul in it. He gives what he can willingly, I know, from a reservoir that seems bottomless.

July 1993

The day we leave Ontario to drive west arrives in some fickle confusion of sun and cloud, humidity and aridness, chill and heat. Appropriate, I decide. Why shouldn't the day hesitate ambivalently before making a firm decision, in much the same way my partner and I have over the past few years? The indecision and hesitancy my partner and I succumb to today seem compressed to me, sculpted, a precise rendering of the larger, broader aimlessness that has plagued us since the newspaper's tragic failure. When I look at the sky this morning, when I peer at the hesitancy of the day, I see myself reflected there. I blend with the day, it blends with me, each trapped inside the other's reflection.

I have decided to go west, and I will not change my mind again. My romantic partner thinks the journey is for the best, too. But less than twelve hours ago, I was of a different mind. Guilt, perhaps, was what afflicted me, or that familiar sense of obligation that brought me to this point in the first place. I arrive at this day no longer certain what in life is worth giving up, what is worth retaining. Last night I imagined I was standing at the edge of a cliff, trying to work up the courage to leap off into the air. Would I plummet or fly? I wondered. And, worse yet, which alternative seemed more attractive to me? Last night I wasn't sure.

I suppose some part of me knew that I would go out west as planned. But this morning it feels less like I'm going because I want to than because I've said I would and now feel obliged to keep my word. My partner's avowal that this trip should be something I do strictly for myself doesn't help to lessen this sense of obligation. And my agreement to take on an elderly travelling companion has squashed any sense of freedom or spontaneity that might once have attached themselves to this voyage. The whimsy inherent in my original scheme has long since been replaced by the burden of responsibility.

My partner and I talked about this last night.

"After what you've been through, you need a spiritual quest," she argued stubbornly.

"I wish you'd come with me."

"I can't right now," she said.

"Why not?"

I thought she'd mention her children again, all of them too old to live with her in the small apartment she has rented in the city, deep inside its slums. After the failure of the newspaper, she was left jobless, too, and now must live in a much less expensive part of the city.

"You regroup in your way. I have to regroup in mine."

Whatever the cause of last night's uncertainty, I have managed to establish some sort of shaky resolve, although traces of doubt still linger in the back of my mind. The residue of confusion that still gnaws at me is reflected in the hastily packed boxes and displaced furniture that litters the farmhouse in which my partner and I have lived for the past year or so. None of the group gathered here this morning needs to be so completely surrounded by disarray — not me, not my partner, not two of her children who are here to help with the move, perhaps not even Lupus. All of our respective futures seem to be in doubt somehow. Everyone is unsure.

The cohort I will be escorting out west has telephoned already to tell me that it will be another two or three hours before he finishes packing up his things. His call came in barely under the wire. With cold efficiency, Bell Canada shut down our telephone service, as we had instructed them to.

While all the confusion of moving is going on, Lupus wanders from room to room — each space echoing more profoundly as its contents are emptied into a rented truck — leaving vapour trails of old dung in his wake. Yesterday he rolled in cow shit, and although I bathed him last night he remains insistently aromatic. Even in the midst of all my sadness and confusion, I'm aware that when we get out on the road together, I'm going to have to open the windows wide to deal with the smell. Lupus may be pleased with his scent, but it remains tragically overpowering as far as my human sensibilities are concerned.

The house is gradually emptied. By mid-afternoon the

various items it housed are packed inside a rented truck. The truck idles in the yard, younger, stronger men than I loitering just outside its doors, waiting for my partner and I to conclude our emotionally inept so-longs. Lupus waits not far away, chained to a small tree. Everything I'm taking west — camping gear, food supplies, pens and paper — lies piled by my waiting car. There's too much, I fear. I don't know how I'll be able to pack it all inside when my overdue travelling companion finally arrives.

"I'll call you," I tell my partner. "I'm just looking for a place for us to begin again."

She doesn't say anything. She is crying.

A few moments later everything is done. The truck leaves our yard, negotiates the long driveway, and then fades down the highway into the distance towards Kingston, vanishing over a hill. It occurs to me that the time for equivocation is now past. Alone, I stand leaning against the car, Lupus reposing on the lawn nearby. We wait for the man we are taking west with us, who is now several hours late.

When my travelling companion finally arrives, I have to repack his car, which looks like a messy room more than a vehicle that is about to embark on an expedition. His move out of his apartment took much longer than he expected, which is why he is so late. He seems panicky and confused about the journey we are about to embark upon. While I have sorted his things in his car for him, he stresses he'll want to do it again tomorrow, more to his satisfaction. This is bound to slow us down, but perhaps we'll be able to make up some of the lost time farther down the road. I hope so; we have a very long way to go.

My best friend expected us to arrive at his cottage near Haliburton by mid-afternoon, but it is early evening by the time we finally make it. My friend is there to greet us when we pull into his yard. I introduce him to my travelling companion. I make my apologies, and my friend takes my travelling companion on a tour of the grounds. We all make our way to the dock and stand there contemplating Wolfe Lake. I have stood here many times, but today is much different. This time I am here to say goodbye.

We hear the splash as Lupus dives into the lake. When we turn, we see him swimming towards a cluster of decorative decoy ducks. He opens his jaws. Then we hear a resounding *clunk* as his teeth close around floating wood and paint. We laugh. Visibly embarrassed, Lupus turns around and swims quickly for the shore.

After a late dinner, an evening of relaxed conversation drifts innocuously away. Soon it's late, after midnight. My best friend and I sit in the warm darkness of his screened-in deck. Lupus sleeps nearby, the aroma of cow dung now exacerbated by the odour of wet fur. My best friend's wife, two young children, and my travelling companion have all retired for the night, so we speak in hushed tones. There are a number of things to say.

"You and Lupus should be making this trip alone," my best friend says.

"Yeah," I admit. "But I felt responsible."

"Where's he going?"

"He's going to live in Kelowna. I'm hoping to be there in three weeks."

"I don't know," my friend muses. "You could probably make it in two weeks, even less, on your own. He's going to slow you down."

"I hope not," I reply, although I'm already feeling some of the folly in our mission now that it's underway.

"So what's the plan?" my best friend wants to know. "I mean what's the ultimate goal?"

"Start over again out west," I say, explaining how I hope to find a place for my partner and me in the mountains. She can join me there once I get settled.

My friend is silent for a time. "She won't do it," he remarks at last.

"What makes you say that?" I ask.

"If she was going to go out west, she'd be with you now."

I realize that he has bluntly voiced a conclusion I have refused to let myself come to on my own.

"No, she'll come out west," I argue weakly.

"I hope you're right," he says, although I can hear the dubiousness in his voice. My friend and I have a long history together. When it comes to my romantic attachments, he has often been quite right. I am usually wrong. I fervently hope this time the pattern will be broken.

We stay at the cottage one day longer than expected. My travelling companion admits he's rather tired, that he didn't sleep well the previous night. But we're off early on the day we finally depart. We drive towards Grundy Lake Provincial Park, south of Sudbury. There we clumsily pitch camp. I help my companion put up his tent before I erect my own. He's in a bit of a state about what lousy campers we are. Tolerating his royal "we" for the moment, I assure him that we'll get better at camping with practice.

I've bought Lupus a can of dog food at a small store along the way, a brand I do not recognize. I feed him while our own food cooks on the Coleman at one end of the picnic table. Lupus sniffs at his food for a moment, then picks ups the dish and carries it over to a small pile of gravel at the edge of our campsite. There, he flips the dish upside down and empties it. He covers the mess with the gravel and urinates on its grave, carefully avoiding his dish. I watch his antics, bemused, then study him as he returns to the picnic table and throws himself down with a grunt.

"Gee, Loop, a simple 'no, thank you' would have sufficed," I say.

But he just looks at me, satisfied that he has made his point.

We stay an extra day again — my companion seems to need the rest. Apparently he finds driving arduous. My domestic labours seem endless. I walk Lupus in between the various meals I must prepare. I cook while camping in the same way I would at home, meat or chicken, mashed potatoes, a side dish, a salad, even dessert, which my co-traveller especially enjoys. Each meal must be served on time, as my associate has diabetes. He washes the dishes afterwards, in a small plastic tub we keep at the end of the table, reflecting our division of labour.

It rains that night. I like the sound of it pattering on the tent. It's intimate and honest. Lupus dozes on a blanket spread out near my sleeping bag. Each night, when we enter the tent to sleep, he lies down on my sleeping bag, staking his claim to it. We enjoy a playful argument about whose bed belongs to whom, Lupus's howls punctuating my entreaties that he move. It's a game he likes. This debate of where each of us is to sleep will reoccur every night during our trip out west. Both of us will come to appreciate it as a ritual conclusion to each day. There's friendship in it and a predictable certainty. I have never loved an animal the way I love him.

On our way towards Sudbury the following morning, I see a large turkey vulture feeding on some roadkill by the side of the highway. It is the ugliest creature that I have ever seen. The next time we stop for gas, I ask my companion if he noticed it.

"No," he replies vaguely, as if it takes all of his energy just to concentrate on the driving without paying attention to the scenery passing by outside the car. He is focused on the end of the journey rather than the journey itself. I simply like the journey. He is society's status quo. I feel like its resident anarchist.

We stop in Sault Ste. Marie to purchase a tarpaulin because my travelling companion is concerned about how much rain has been falling. He is a smoker, and he frequently opens the top flap of his dome tent to allow the smoke from his cigarette to escape. But when he does, the rain comes in through the flap and soaks his sleeping bag. The solution, he maintains, is a tarp similar to the ones we've seen strung up around the campsites where we've stayed. Not having the heart to argue, I purchase one at a hardware store. It's too large and too heavy for the use my travelling companion wants to put it to, but I'm in a hurry and so am careless about its excessive dimensions. My only immediate feeling is one of relief that I'm able to find a place for it on top of some gear that I carry in my back seat.

We set up camp just north of Sault Ste. Marie on the shores of Lake Superior. The lake teases me by masquerading as an ocean. I have been fascinated by the sea for as long as I can remember, and this fascination has kept me away from it for much of my life. I might fall so deeply in love with the sea that I would risk my own destruction. I hate this fear; it goes against my nature. It reflects the kind of cautious, practical thinking that I've not yet been able to disavow.

My travelling companion decides to visit a sprawling gift shop a few miles up the highway while I take Lupus for a walk. We see him driving by us several times on the network of campsite roadways, obviously lost. At last I flag him down and give him directions to the exit. He's embarrassed and frustrated. I tell him his confusion could happen to anyone. But after he is gone, I fret about his puzzlement and about the resentment I feel having to continually look out for his well-being. Before this journey west, he was a self-reliant man. Now that we are constantly together, he has changed. His needs are increasingly left up to me to satisfy. It leaves me little time to myself. That evening, before the sun goes down, I find an hour or so of peace on an empty range of sand dunes by the lakeshore. Here I break the park's rules and let Lupus off his leash. We run and chase one another, my various worries retreating for a time as Lupus and I play.

Feeling newly expansive and hopeful, I telephone my partner and offer to backtrack several hundred miles to pick her up so that she can accompany the three of us on our journey. As a suggestion, it's logistically impractical, but I believe with creative dedication I can figure out a way to squeeze her into my car. Nonetheless, she declines.

It is the last time I suggest she make this trip with me. It is the last time she tells me that she loves me. It is the last hopeful conversation we ever have.

Lupus and I are exploring a nature trail in Sleeping Giant Provincial Park near Thunder Bay when we come face to face with a full-grown doe. We are in deep woods here, and we have just taken a wooden bridge across a brook, rounding a sharp bend in the path. The deer seems to materialize there like a wraith, so much so that it doesn't look real at first. It's too calm, too self-assured. Shouldn't the sound of our approach have frightened it off?

I shorten Lupus's leash by wrapping it several times around my hand, but he doesn't pull very hard. The deer comes to a halt on the trail and stares at Lupus, who stands barely six feet away. Lupus stares back at the doe while I glance back and forth at both of them, mesmerized by their stillness. For a full five minutes none of us moves, after Lupus has sat down. He never stops gazing at the deer in philosophical reflection. I have no idea what motivates these animals to scrutinize each other this way. Are they merely curious or is there a conflict here over which one is the intruder and should give way?

Finally, the doe turns and begins to saunter slowly up the trail the way it came. Lupus, now wanting to give chase, begins to tug fiercely on his leash, but I am ready for this and hold on tight. I stand there with Lupus for another few minutes to make certain the deer has had time to get away before we continue walking.

That same night a flying squirrel soars to the trunk of a tree by our picnic table, a few inches from my head. Lupus gets up and comes to stare at the intruder until it disappears again.

"Whaddyuh think, Loop? Do you think we should live in the woods?"

But he only glances at me, dubiously perhaps, recognizing my whimsy for what it is: a failure to acknowledge where he and I might ultimately have to live.

It takes us more than eight days to get out of Ontario. I rationalize this extended period of time as a by-product of my home province's large size. But the truth is that our slow progress is the result of the pace my travelling companion has managed to set for us. I've allowed him to do this, it's *his* journey now.

We stay two nights in Manitoba. On the second night, several inches of rain fall. I have not strung up our giant tarpaulin because the campsite is too small. In the morning my tent is an island in a small lake of rainfall. But all my gear is dry. Not so my companion's sleeping bag, which is soaked through.

"Did you have the flap open again?" I ask him, as I prepare breakfast. He doesn't answer but I know he's wishing I had found a way to put up the tarp.

I bite back my anger and frustration. "When we get to Saskatchewan, we'll hang up your sleeping bag in the sunshine," I say.

"If it ever stops raining."

I'm too annoyed to say anything. Instead I point west to where the sullen clouds are giving way to little pockets of blue sky. I don't say anything. I want him to notice it for himself.

If he recognizes the break in the weather, though, he doesn't say so.

We drive the first few hundred miles of Canada's great prairies. I like their earthy greens and browns and the grain elevators that seem to burst forth from the land as though they occurred there naturally. But my companion is fed up with the flatness of the land and tells me so when we stop for lunch. I don't know what to say. The geography isn't my fault.

Before we resume driving, I consult my map. "Next stop," I say, "the Qu'Appelle Valley."

It's sunny now and warm. My friend's mood improves. "I can dry my sleeping bag," he says with near enthusiasm.

Not long after we leave Manitoba, we get off the Trans-Canada and veer north. A few miles later we leave the prairie flatness behind and enter a different world, the lakes and greenery of the valley. For me, entering the valley is like leaving one dimension and coming upon another. The prairie, so sprawling, so full of horizon, gives way to the valley carved into it like some desert oasis. I am moved by the contrast; my spirits are lifted. Someday, I tell myself, I must travel the entire planet. I owe the planet this. It is there to be explored, it would be a waste not to do so.

I tell Lupus of my plan and invite him along. He sits on the passenger seat, sniffing at the open window. But at the sound of my voice he turns to gaze at me, giving me a canine shrug of casual agreement. I reach out to stroke him behind the ears and scratch his neck. He puts up with this. It's part of the price he must pay to travel this world with me, a man frequently compelled to render love with restless fingers. I'm beginning to believe we'll always be together, Lupus and I, howling at a common moon.

The park at which we stop, Crooked Lake, operates on the honour system. We tuck our camping fees for two nights into an envelope and push this into a slot in a waiting box. The place is virtually deserted, so we have our choice of sites. We find one we like on the shores of the lake. It's warm, sunny, and peaceful. There is a wondrous solitude here that I relish. Sometimes I feel that, if solitude were alcohol, I would go on a reckless bender; I have not been alone enough. For once I am glad we'll be staying two nights. I would have stayed here two nights whether or not I had my tired and impatient charge in tow.

At dusk I become aware of a distant, persistent hum. I have been so happy since arriving at this place—building a fire, cooking an elaborate dinner, gazing at the lake lapping against its shoreline—that this unusual noise has been slow to penetrate my consciousness. It sounds like the distant drone of tractor-trailers wheeling down a busy freeway, but that cannot be the source; even the Trans-Canada is too far from here for traffic noises to be audible.

My travelling companion hears it too, but neither of us can make out where it's coming from. The sound is insistent and unbroken, and it seems to come from everywhere.

I look up at the sky, which is now adopting a shade of deeper blue. That is when I discover the source of the endless hum. I call to my travelling companion and point into the heavens.

"Oh, my," he says.

A few yards over our heads, a swarm of mosquitoes is conducting a colossal dogfight with an array of larger insects that prey upon them. There must be billions of them. Reflected against the sky, this humming blanket of tiny bodies is loud and threatening, a writhing, endlessly twitching gauze against the darkening blue of the sky.

My travelling companion sits down beside me at our picnic table. "Sooner or later they're all going to come down here to feed on human flesh."

"I expect so," I reply.

"I'm going to bed before they show up."

"Sounds like a plan," I say.

Not long after darkness falls, however, the eerie hum vanishes entirely. Instead of descending upon our campsite like some biblical plague, it seems as if the insects have just flown off. Lupus grows restless and stands at the doorway of our tent while I read by the light of a lantern I've positioned just outside the mesh.

"What is it, Loop?"

I hear something tearing into the garbage bag of scraps and grocery wrappers that I neglectfully left near our picnic table. I leash Lupus and grab my flashlight before cautiously emerging from the tent to investigate.

I catch a glimpse of the skunk as it retreats into a stand of shrubs a few feet from my travelling companion's tent.

"Are you awake?" I call.

"Yes."

"Well, stay in your tent. There's a skunk hiding in the bushes just outside your door."

"Oh, terrific," he replies.

Lupus is disinterested in the skunk and lies down by the picnic table while I gather up our garbage and lock it in the car. Lupus doesn't get excited about nocturnal visitors. He seems to bring an inherent wisdom to camping, and I am grateful for it. But around two a.m., I awake to the sound of Lupus whining. He is standing at the mesh by the tent's door. I roll over onto my stomach and peer outside. The moon has risen full and perched itself on the horizon of the lake. It's as big as a dinner plate, our campsite awash in reflected light. At first I don't see anything. Then, suddenly, something large and clearly misshapen wanders across the face of the moon. Lupus sees it too. It's not a wolf, but it doesn't look like a dog either. Mostly it resembles a hyena — short, deformed back legs, a powerful and large front torso. It must be a dog, but, as it stands partially revealed by the light of the moon, it is one of the largest, strangest dogs I've ever seen.

Before I can get a good look at it, it's gone, disappearing along the shore of the lake.

Lupus remains on duty for another ten minutes or so before giving up his post and lying down again on his blanket. I am comforted by the acuteness of his senses. I trust that he will sound any alarm I might require to warn me of imminent danger.

On the move again the next day, we drive through an abating rainfall towards Buffalo Pound Provincial Park, farther west along the Qu'Appelle Valley. It's clearing up by the time we locate our allotted campsite at the edge of a small stand of trees. I chain Lupus to our picnic table and set about finding a means to hang the massive tarpaulin my travelling companion insists we'll need as cover in case there's any more rain. To erect such a large piece of plastic, I am going to have to climb each of four trees. I am standing contemplating the immensity of this chore when a young man crosses the road from his campsite and offers to shimmy up the trees that, due to my age and lack of practice, would be impossible for me to climb. He's as agile as a monkey and it doesn't take him long. We conduct a debriefing session after he completes his mission, our entire campsite now draped in blue plastic.

"Your tarp's too big," he informs me.

"Yeah, I know," I say.

"Covers the whole campsite."

"Yeah."

"Besides, it's supposed to clear up."

This time I merely nod.

I suppose we could dwell much longer on the tarp, its failures, and the weather I can't read, but he begins to admire Lupus, who, as always, exudes his endless magnetism. Eventually my good Samaritan departs, dismissing still more gratitude from me with a careless wave of his hand. With the tarpaulin now in place, my travelling companion and I begin to unload our gear from our cars. Lupus, tied to the leg of a picnic table by a twenty-foot chain, pokes around the campsite sniffing here and there at shrubs and trees and turf. I allow Lupus to explore while I continue to get us settled. A few moments pass, then I am alerted by the unmistakable drone of a very large number of insects. I swivel around in time to see Lupus extract his head from a knothole in one of the nearby trees. The noise makes it clear that he has inadvertently stumbled upon a nest of yellow jackets.

There's a moment of calm, and then the wasps declare war on us. I shout the alarm to my travelling companion, who dashes for his car, climbs inside, and rolls his window up. Lupus, trapped at the end of his chain, is fighting back. I can hear the click of his teeth as he bites down on the wasps. I race towards him and into the fray, intending to disconnect him so we can retreat to our car. Soon, though, we're both doing battle, seriously outnumbered. I don't know how many wasps we kill before we finally manage to make it to the car. Dozens, I suppose. Lupus killing them in his jaws, me pulling them out of his coat where they've embedded themselves in search of exposed flesh. I reach into his fur and crush them in my fingers like a dutiful simian mother removing lice from the flesh of her children.

After the carnage abates, I take some time to assess the damage. Lupus has been stung several times around the face. The swelling is significant. He looks deformed, misshapen, like the victim of some tragic genetic mutation. No damage around the eyes, though. Mostly he seems fine. And I am amazed that I was not stung at all. Once I've completed my inspection, I drive to the park office to report the incident.

It turns out that the wasps' nest is located deep in the trunk of the tree. It will take two maintenance men several days to remove it. The park ranger condemns the campsite and allots us another one. We repack our cars. As a final chore, I cut the damned tarpaulin down.

By the next afternoon, Lupus has completely recovered from his war with the wasps. I noticed with some surprise that his swelling was gone within a few hours, even though he had been stung several times. Now he and I climb a steep, barren hill not far from our campsite. Since we are quite some distance from the nearest civilization, I gratefully unhook his leash to let him run. By now I am used to his physical prowess, but I am nonetheless nonplussed by his ability to spring up and down steep sections of this high, demanding hill, while I puff and snort, my feet stumbling clumsily on rocks, sand, and grass. As I make my awkward way up the incline, Lupus bounds ahead of me.

When I am perhaps halfway up the hill, I notice him waiting for me several yards ahead.

"You having fun, Loop?" I call up to him.

The next moment he's charging at me at full speed. I try to step aside — I'm familiar with this game — but he anticipates my manoeuvre and hits me on the left knee. Down I go like a cliff-edge tree that has finally stopped scrabbling to remain upright. I lie there a moment or two, stunned, relieved that I have managed to keep from rolling all the way down the hill. Lupus approaches and stares down at me with an expression on his face that resembles a grin.

"You bugger," I say, once I've caught my breath. But he just grins more broadly, like the badass he is.

When we finally gain the top of the hill, I find a sandy plateau and sit down to enjoy the day, a wall of rock and sand at my back. It's sunny and warm and silent, and much of Buffalo Pound stretches out towards a broad horizon I can almost clutch and hold in my hand. There's an abandoned animal's lair a few feet above my head and Lupus leaps up and claims it as his own. He lies on this rock shelf and gazes out over the panorama in front of him. We stay here for more than an hour, thinking our private thoughts. Lupus, I suspect, calmly counts his blessings. I, on the other hand, do what so many humans do: I sort through all the missed opportunities in my past, which, had I not ignored them at the time, might have brought me to this place when I was a younger man.

On our way back down the hill, Lupus dashes ahead of me and, before I can connect him to his leash, disappears at full gallop into a large stand of trees at the bottom. I call after him several times, but he does not come back. By the time I reach the trees, he is nowhere to be found. I am fearful that, for reasons of his own, he has decided to run away. I hurry the last several hundred yards to our campsite, prepared to announce to my travelling companion that Lupus has disappeared.

But when I get there, I find Lupus lying peacefully at the threshold of our tent.

"I thought he'd taken off," I admit.

My travelling companion shrugs. "He showed up a few minutes ago, drank a gallon of water, and lay down in front of your tent."

I shake my head and connect him to the chain looped around the leg of our picnic table. I stroke him behind the ears. I am relieved that he hasn't lost patience with me, that he hasn't decided to leave me behind because I can't keep up with him.

We don't so much as glimpse the buffalo for which the park is named. We drive to the lookout tower before sunset that same day, but the buffalo hide in the arroyos and gullies where it is cool and private.

"No buffalo for you, Loop," I say before we depart. He doesn't care, of course. Not burdened by expectation, he doesn't succumb to disappointment. Lack of expectation, I suppose, is the true meaning of ignorance as bliss.

We spend two nights at Cypress Hills on the Saskatchewan-Alberta border before heading towards my brother's home in the suburbs north of Calgary. Our stay at Cypress Hills is uneventful, although I've become sick and tired of erecting what I am now convinced is the world's largest tarpaulin, only for it not to rain.

As we cross the last section of prairie on our way to Calgary, my travelling companion keeps falling asleep at the wheel of his car. It's mid-morning. Ever since this journey began, without being consciously aware of it, I've repeatedly checked my rear-view and side mirrors to keep an eye on the car behind me. This morning, on more than one occasion when I've glanced in my rear-view, I've noticed his car weaving into the passing lane, then veering back again. Medicine Hat, where we intend to stop for lunch, is still some distance away and, alarmed, I pull over to the side of the road to make certain my travelling companion is all right. When we meet on the shoulder beside my car to talk, he admits with a curious calm that he keeps dozing off behind the wheel. We're in the middle of nowhere, and if coffee is a solution, I'm going to have to brew it on the Coleman here at the side of the road. But he declines my offer, and we finally drive on. A little farther along the highway we find a restaurant. It is lunchtime, so we stop there for a rest and a bite to eat earlier than planned. I've made this brief drive anxiously. Operating one car while another veers perilously from side to side in the rear-view is the epitome of helplessness, as far as I'm concerned.

We stay with my brother in Calgary for a couple of days. It rains, for the most part. My brother claims that in good weather the Rocky Mountains are visible in the distance from his back balcony. In the mist and rain, we must take his word for it. Rain is one thing, rainy suburbs are much worse. The houses move in on one another lecherously, partially hidden by the mist. So I'm anxious to get going, to be on the move again, even in the rain.

When we depart the Calgary area, we are committed to our shortest day of driving. We intend to stay at Banff, even though it's nearby and to do so will delay us further from reaching our final destination. The day is crisp and clear. We can see the mountains, virtually the moment we set out. They are bright grey and blue and white, the way my brother said they would be.

"It's like driving into a postcard," my travelling companion says when we stop for lunch.

I nod enthusiastically. I'm relieved that something in our travels has appealed to him at last.

Sometimes I think Lupus is a magnet for phenomena. Although I should have come to this conclusion much earlier, it strikes me as I stand on a cliff overlooking one of the park lakes. Here, I begin to catalogue the events that led me to this assumption. How many incidents have there been with large birds of prey, for example? Three? Four? Even back east there have been stories I've told, strange moments with giant birds that have filled me briefly with wonder.

But this afternoon in Banff is the first time that I pull the threads together, that my mind opens widely enough to wonder what causes the relationship between Lupus and me and various birds of prey. Are we being told to soar and swoop through life? Are we being advised to abandon our snail's pace along life's conventional highways?

This time an eagle dashes across the lake towards us. Even though it has not yet closed on us, I can see it carries something large in its talons. I glance at Lupus and see that he has spotted it, too. He sits beside my left leg, mesmerized by the sight. The eagle flies directly at us. I force myself to stand my ground. Then, seconds later, the bird soars up just over my head, so close I can glimpse the markings on the fish trapped in its talons. I turn, but the eagle veers away. Soon it vanishes into the trees. I stand there for a moment, finally realizing I must take a breath again, I must remember to breathe in my awe, to keep breathing in the wonder I hope to find in my future. Eventually Lupus and I move on, still following the same trail away from the lake and deeper into the woods. I hear a woman gasp as I turn a sharp bend in the trail, following Lupus around the corner. I see a couple in their early sixties, both of whom have stepped off the pathway in alarm.

"Hello," I say to them.

They are looking at Lupus. But now that they've noticed his leash, their relief is palpable.

"I thought it was a wolf," the woman remarks. She has a British accent.

I stop for a moment. "Well, maybe a little bit," I say.

"He's yours?"

"Yes."

They want to get going, to move away from here. Even knowing Lupus is on his leash and apparently belongs to me, they are nervous and agitated by the way Lupus has materialized on this wooded trail as its unexpected delegate.

"Sorry we startled you."

"I thought it was a wolf," she repeats in a tone that is vaguely accusatory.

I don't know what else to say, so I walk off without another word.

Later that same afternoon, Lupus and I retreat to our tent for a short nap before dinner. When I awake, I open the tent flaps to emerge into the daylight, but notice Lupus hesitating at the opening, as though gauging how best to make his exit. He starts to move out of the tent, then veers sharply to his left and disappears from my view. Still half asleep, and puzzled by this,

I poke my head outside, then lurch back inside again. A full-grown elk stands in front of my tent. Now I understand. To exit the way he usually does, Lupus would have had to go between the elk's legs, directly underneath its imposing undercarriage.

I must wait a couple of minutes for the elk to move away before I can gingerly leave my tent. I chain Lupus to the picnic table, although he is merely lying at the edge of our campsite, watching what I have now discovered is a large group of elk grazing through our sprawling suburbia of tents. The campsite is transformed into a carnival: the elk are surrounded by excited clusters of tourists snapping photographs, everyone talking at once in hoarse, delighted whispers.

My travelling companion sits at the picnic table, no doubt waiting for his dinner. He gestures at the elk. "Looks like we're going to have to make more salad," he says with a grin.

This is the friend I used to know, the one with a sense of humour. I am glad his good nature has returned, even if it is only temporary.

That evening I watch large magpies and ravens glide through the trees. They are fat and relentless. I recall hearing them described as flying pigs.

After the sun goes down, park vehicles patrol the campsites every few minutes. Word spreads from tent to tent. "Bears. There've been sightings of bears." I sit at the picnic table in the dark. The patrols continue long into the night, but I don't see any bears.

"Just you and me soon, Loop," I say, as I often do, sharing an optimism with him that, to my ears, at least, sounds vaguely surprising.

February 1993

The two personal tragedies that take place in my life in the winter of 1993 occur almost simultaneously, separated by only a couple of days. And in my perception they seem catastrophic. In the thrall of my two separate tragedies, I can see only one outcome: I am going to leave this world a failure.

I am in the hospital, lying on my back on a hard table. I wear only a hospital gown and I am cold, the victim of a draft that permeates the room. Above me I glimpse a large screen that reveals the streams of arteries around my heart. It clunks in protest as the doctor shifts it here and there to find the spot he must enlarge to increase blood flow to my heart. I don't think much. I'm too tired to think.

I've been here before. This is my second angioplasty. I was diagnosed with angina more than a year ago. I've suffered one heart attack. The damage, they said, was insignificant, but everyone agrees I am too young to be suffering from a heart condition. Everyone agrees that I have been working myself to death. They drugged me to calm me, perhaps an hour or so ago, but the fear I feel at my circumstances — not so much the procedure itself, but my future now that my health has been shattered — fills me with silent dread. Normally I am the kind of man who, if kept awake during a medical procedure, would quip back and forth with the doctor and three nurses here in this theatre. I like people and conversation, and it would make me feel brave. But doubts about my future, what will become of me economically after I return home, are so powerful they silence me.

I must lie very still and can see little of this cavernous room. The camera above me, the doctor, the nearby nurses, my own naked body covered in a sheet on this narrow table. In the distance a small group of medical students observes the procedure. I've been told they are there, and I caught a glimpse of them before the angioplasty got underway, but I can't see them now that I must remain immobile. One aspect of this procedure is relatively new: they are going to insert a stent, a metal bridge, into my artery to keep it open in the future, to convey blood to my struggling heart.

I feel a familiar surge of pain in the left side of my chest that shoots caustically down my arm. I am told I am having a heart attack, but they assure me that I am going to be all right. I hear these words as if from a discreet distance; they don't appear to arrive from someone speaking, but rather seem to inhabit the air all around me. The people in this room are prepared for heart attacks during an angioplasty. I *am* all right. Something, probably nitroglycerin or morphine, is injected with a syringe into one of the various cables connected to my veins, and the pain slips away. But they want to know the instant it returns, should I feel it again. This was not an emergency procedure. When we scheduled it, the doctor explained the risks to me. Hooked up to various IVs and monitors, with hospital staff buzzing all around me, the doctor's explanation now seems somewhat pale and hollow.

The doctors finish the procedure and I return to my room in intensive care. Here I am reconnected to the array of dials, monitors, and machines that allow the medical staff to keep an eye on me. I must lie in one position for the prescribed six hours so that I do not bleed from the artery in my leg that served as the entry point for the doctors to explore my heart. Eventually, the doctor comes to see me, and I am told that the angioplasty was a success. The slight heart attack during the procedure occurred because the repairs to the section of artery in this difficult location briefly closed another arterial opening. I imagine this opening gasping. I see it as a mouth, as a windpipe trying to catch a breath.

Over the next few days, there are conversations between me and the medical staff. Some of these take the form of outraged lamentations. "You're only forty-four years old," the doctors say. "How did you come to be in this state of health?"

I don't know how to answer them. I have been pushing all my life, as if I had something to prove. I'm not sure I'll ever learn how to stop.

My partner comes to see me sporadically in the days that

follow. She is distressed by the hospital environment and by what is happening to me here. She doesn't like hospitals, and after five or ten minutes she flees, until the next occasion when some vague concoction of love or guilt compels her to come and see me again. I think I know why she is afraid. She shares my worries about the future, and she harbours the same sense of failure. If we were completely honest, I think we'd both have to admit to feeling as if all our hard work on the newspaper project had come to nothing more than this: a man perhaps permanently broken in a hospital bed, exhausted and depleted, with no place left to go. No wonder she stays away. She, too, has a life she must sort out of the wreckage of what we have lost together.

I am not lonely, though. Not really. I am acquainted with the doctors and nurses here in cardiac care. They remember me. I am the one they thought was crazed. I know that they recall my earlier stay in intensive care, after my first heart attack, connected to machines and bags of drugs, to screens and dials and buzzers. On my first day I asked if it would be all right if someone from my newspaper brought my computer to my bedside, because I had work to do. They turned me down with some astonished mixture of anger and amusement. I sensed briefly then what it must be like to be considered insane. People don't understand the meaning of your words, they don't grasp the nature of your most intense fear. Because they do not share it. On that occasion, the only fear they were willing to acknowledge was the fear I might have for my health. But the terror preoccupying me had nothing to do with the fragile state of my physical being. The real terror that obsessed me was terror over the survival of the newspaper, and that was left for me to endure alone. At some point in my earlier ordeal, I was told that the time had come for me to feel responsible for myself and not for everyone else. But I didn't listen. To focus on my own well-being would have seemed selfish then. I had been brought up to believe that life is sacrifice, that the obligations we embrace, the larger and more numerous the better, define our value, our purpose. We receive our rewards in heaven, I was told. What they failed to add was that first we must nobly self-destruct.

The other disaster is the newspaper ceasing operation. A scant few days before the angioplasty that would keep me in hospital for a week, we have to move all of our possessions out of the office we occupied for nearly four years. Closures such as this one take place under cover of darkness. In the middle of the night, we skulk to a waiting truck, carrying files, computer equipment, desks and chairs, hiding from the shame of such a public failure.

I am seriously ill. So is the project I founded nearly four years ago when it became clear that my communications consulting business could not support me, my partner, and her children. She was unable to secure a teaching position, but wished to stay in Kingston. I convinced myself that a larger business — a weekly newspaper — would satisfy my obligations to my new family.

For a couple of years now, the newspaper and I have been owed between thirty and fifty thousand dollars every single day. The exhaustion of endlessly chasing this money has felled both me and the newspaper. I have grown bitter about the world of business and the accommodation it provides for people who don't pay their bills. Big business rationalizes and legitimizes theft. Words like *entrepreneur, businessman, chief executive officer* are to me only euphemisms for socially acceptable banditry, authorized gangsterism, and a paradigm that makes avarice and brazen self-interest respectable.

It's early February, and I am crushed. I don't know who I am. I don't know where I am. Most of all, I don't know why I am. I don't know how, after working so hard for so long, I have come to be in this place in time, defined mostly by self-loathing and disappointment. Or why, when I need to recover my health, the conventional world I've tried so hard to please glares down on me in finger-wagging judgment. I don't feel like a man with thoughts or dreams. I feel like a felon. Society has given me my opportunity, and it wants me to know I have abused its gift. Even if I repent somehow, I must wear my mark of Cain forever, so everyone can see it and know the reason I must be shunned.

For a few weeks, I hide away in our home a few miles outside Kingston. I don't want to see anyone. I don't even want to see *myself.* For nearly four years I have exhausted my physical, spiritual, and mental resources. In four years I have never worked less than ninety hours during any given week. I recall one week when my working hours totalled one hundred and twenty-three. I have deprived myself of sleep for years, and I have ignored my health. I have eaten irregularly, only when I had the chance, and exercise has been sporadic. When ill with colds or the flu, I continued working. Following bilateral hernia surgery, I went to work on my way home from hospital. I have been in hospital several times during the life of the newspaper —once diagnosed with exhaustion—and, as soon as I could arrange it, have escaped to begin abusing myself again. No wonder the ashes of my defeat mingle with those of the newspaper.

This is the situation in which I find myself during the winter that Lupus and I begin to become true companions. We begin to draw close to one another, to become the friends and comrades we will eventually be, during this time of turmoil and defeat.

He has been part of our household for only a few months. When he first came into our lives, he was more affixed to my partner than he was to me. I was chained to the newspaper and didn't have the time to spend with him. But my partner, who was responsible for selling advertising for the newspaper, took him on her calls. He travelled the city streets with her and became a fixture in her car. Now that the newspaper has imploded, however, and we all cower in our home, he becomes more and more my friend. In the days and weeks following the newspaper's demise, Lupus and I transform ourselves into creatures of the night. During this period I stay awake deep into the night. I am afraid that if I succumb to slumber, I will never again wake up, that my life will slip away from me before I am done with it. As harsh and disappointing as being alive seems to be, I despise and fear the thought of giving up, giving way, giving in. So Lupus and I patrol the night while everyone else is asleep. We discover a wondrous world I've never noticed before. This world is wilder than I realized; it belongs more to Lupus than to me.

There are wolves that live in the woods a mile from our house, a large grey male and a smaller red-tinged female. The farmer from whom we rent has told me this. He has seen them on occasion when he has been out working his land. One night that February around two a.m., as Lupus and I depart the house we see one of the wolves about twenty yards away, not far from the garage. It glances at us, then darts off, leaping the fence and vanishing into the night. The wolf is hardly there a second before it disappears, its flight prompted less by alarm than by a need for privacy.

I stand there a long time remarking on what I have just seen, holding on to it, wondering why the wolf's actions made a strange kind of sense to me. Then again, maybe I am just reaching for something to distract me. Maybe I just desperately need something to embrace, something new or different that belongs to me alone.

There is something wild in Lupus I've never seen before in a dog, something that closely resembles the wildness of the wolf I've just witnessed. I wouldn't call it madness, nor even a lack of discipline. No, I witness a fundamental skill he brings to life, a physical superiority that cries *I'm wilderness*. I've seen examples of this wildness in him on several occasions. He finds mice beneath the snow, then eats them. One morning, he nearly snares a rabbit. It is a near miss. Lupus lunges at the small creature at top speed, sending it fleeing into some deep shrubs in a cloud of powdery snow. Lupus is unable to recover from the rabbit's sudden change in direction in time to continue his pursuit. But I am struck by the speed with which he began his attack, the way he moves so silently. It mystifies me. I don't know how he does it. When he runs at full speed, I can't hear him coming. He hardly seems to touch the ground at all, but rather skims the Earth's surface, never making a sound.

One morning a man drives into the yard to have a look at our roof. I am outside waiting for him; the man who owns our house told me to expect him. I greet the roofer as he climbs out of the cab of his truck. Lupus, ever curious, peers over the peak of a spotlessly snowy slope a couple of hundred yards away. Seeing we have company, he dashes in our direction.

Running at top speed, he is silent. I have the sense that I am watching a movie without sound. The man glimpses him out of the corner of his eye, however, and, turning his head, sees Lupus bearing down on us.

"Jesus," he cries in alarm. "That's a fucking wolf."

Before I can reassure him, he dashes for his truck and scrambles back into the cab, closing the door behind him. As Lupus pulls up by my side, I call out to the man in the truck to let him know that he is safe, that Lupus is our dog. But the man will not leave his truck until Lupus and his crazy master have both gone inside.

As winter continues, I become more and more receptive to the wilderness surrounding us. I become sensitive to the wildness in Lupus that seems to reflect what has escaped my notice until now. He is the conduit for this new perception. As we spend more and more time together, tangible examples of the wilderness present themselves.

I sight a large hawk one night while Lupus and I are outside. I notice it before Lupus does, looming a few yards away on a bare tree branch in the corner of our yard. As it cautiously departs, spreading its wings to abandon its perch for the starlit sky, Lupus spots it and half-heartedly gives chase until the bird is out of sight. We are also visited that winter by a great Arctic snowy owl. Rarely spotted this far south, the owl is the largest bird I have ever seen. I must consult some field guides in my library before I truly believe what I have seen.

Birds of prey are not the only wild animals Lupus and I encounter that remarkable winter. I become aware of a pack of coyotes that yip and bark at night some distance from our house. Standing there in the darkness, I hear them often. I have no idea how many there are, although I suspect there could be a dozen. One night, again around two a.m., the coyotes begin their crying, sounding much closer than usual. Lupus freezes and cocks his head. Squinting into the deep darkness, I try to make out the coyotes' position and decide they are somewhere in the vicinity of where our long lane connects with the highway. Lupus has come to a similar decision. Without warning, he darts down the lane and disappears into the night. There is no moon. Although the night is clear, I cannot see anything. I can only hear. Then, abruptly, the coyotes' cries cease.

"Lupus," I call sternly. "Come here. Right now!"

I am not certain what the coyotes will do if Lupus dashes into their midst. Will he frighten them off or, given confidence by their numbers, will they attack and kill him? Will he join them? Strangely enough, as I hurry down the driveway, hoping I can scare the coyotes off, I recall a Billy Crystal comic routine about coming home to find his dog surrounded by coyotes. One of the coyotes says to the dog, "Hey, pal, wanna be a coyote?" I fret that maybe Lupus does. I keep calling him. The coyotes remain disturbingly silent, like they're waiting out there for Lupus, whether to embrace or kill him, I can't be certain.

"Lupus. Come here!"

Then, with a surprisingly deep gush of relief, I see him, trotting calmly up the lane. I nab him and leash him. I take a deep breath, getting hold of myself, before we turn back towards the house.

"Atta boy, Loop," I say, deeply relieved he came back to me. Only rarely after this do I hear the coyotes cry.

It's spring now, the end of April. My best friend is visiting me, and we have taken Lupus out for a walk, bringing a thermos of coffee along with us. The ice has shattered on the St. Lawrence River and drifts downstream in shimmering fragments. Someone's wooden raft has floated downstream along with the ice and has become caught in a small bay at the edge of the woods on my landlord's property, a short jump from shore. My best friend and I sit on this slightly bobbing raft, drinking coffee from two mugs and exploring what I should do with myself now that my life has been reduced to shambles. Somewhere in the woods behind us, Lupus runs gleefully from tree to tree. I catch a glimpse of him now and then, but the mysterious silence that is his most prevailing characteristic persists. Even here, among last year's leaves and fallen tree branches, he runs without even a whisper to accompany his movement. Then suddenly, unannounced, he lands on the raft. He has leapt soundlessly from the shore to materialize like a demon on the planks between my friend and me. I saw him coming, my friend did not. He cries out in surprise and spills half of his coffee. To him, Lupus has dropped from the sky without making a sound.

"How does he *do* that?" my friend wants to know after he's recovered.

All I can do is shrug. "We should have named him Ghost."

I chase the newspaper's overdue accounts. As I hunt, I am also hunted. While I easily come up with funds to clear up the newspaper's obligations, my personal economic responsibilities are more difficult to alleviate. In the last eight months of the newspaper's existence, I stopped paying myself the subsistence salary that had helped support my partner and the youngest of her four children. As the funds we were owed became more and more elusive, I extended my personal credit. Now that the newspaper is gone, I must seek the money owed to deal with my own debts. Immediately after leaving hospital, I called my personal creditors and explained my dilemma. At first appreciative of my candour, they waited only two weeks before beginning to hound me, which is both pointless and needless. I pay when I collect, after I come up with food and rent.

This problem is exacerbated by the refusal of an insurance company to live up to its obligations over a disability policy I have owned for a number of years. Despite a series of letters from the herd of doctors currently looking after me, the company insists I am well enough to work. Backed by the support of my doctors, I call the company's head office to dispute their view. "So sue us," the representative retorts, knowing full well I do not have the resources to do so.

In the meantime, the money-grubbing siege continues. I personally visit the various businesses that owe us money. Some of them are staggeringly abject about their refusal. "But you're no longer in business," I'm told.

"The money's still owed," I counter.

They shrug and turn away, customers I have known for years, whom I have considered colleagues. They gesture without shame in the direction of the door. At home, meanwhile, bill collectors leave their complaints and accusations on our answering machine.

The strangest aspect of this ordeal, however, is the way the community has grown silent now that the newspaper is gone.

Once enthusiastic about the publication, grateful for the way it helped bring the community together, the municipality's politicians and heads of business are suddenly out of touch. Once again, everyone behaves as if the newspaper and I were one and the same. With the newspaper now dead, in the eyes of the community I am dead, too. Bill collectors are the only voices to be heard on the tinny tape inside our answering machine. Regardless of everything I've accomplished in the past, the ethics and dedication with which I've approached my life, the prevailing question put to me now is: "What have you done for us lately?"

As spring slips into summer, I hold periodic yard sales to raise funds for food and rent. I watch possessions leave our yard for a fraction of what they are worth. Yet, while I feel exploited by our circumstances, I am strangely unmoved by these losses. I have never been a materialistic person. I have always feared owning too much; possessions have a way of intruding upon personal freedom. And yet, up to this point, I accepted the conventional belief that material commodities are the basis of our security and the proof of our achievements. This belief is now evaporating quickly, and I realize it never had much substance to begin with. Things come and go too easily, while I remain. In the end I am the one with substance, not the microwave or the extra coffee table or the cordless telephone, or any of the things we thought we needed.

As the weeks pass, my partner and I try at times to regroup. But we are exhausted by our mutual wasted effort and by the guilty verdict that has been imposed on us now that our business is defunct. We drift, separately for the most part. Neither of us has the strength to console the other. And so our partnership develops fractures. We are distracted from resuming the intimacy in our relationship by the severity of our economic needs and by the fatigue we suffer in he wake of the newspaper's closing. Having invested so much time and energy in this project —four years of long hours and periods of waxing and waning frustration — we have no energy left to devote to a unified remedy for our losses. These losses, though shared, are also private, unique to each of us. I seek out my solution, she contemplates her own. I spend much of my time with Lupus, she seeks out a clan of female friends. I want to write during this period. She wants to return to teaching. Each of us, I suspect, tends to blame the other for embarking on this newspaper project. In both cases, it interrupted our own separate plans. We try to heal our wounds intermittently. And, for a time, we believe we can. It will take a few more months for both of us — first her, then me — to decide we cannot restore the partnership we once enjoyed. I assume much of the responsibility for the widening gap between us.

Yet, yet . . .

. . . there is Lupus. And the strange, heretical exhilaration of simply being alive.

Several hundred yards from the house, high ground gives way to a large, sprawling acreage separating our property from the woods at the river's edge. Lupus and I walk this field on our way into the woods most days. A creek divides this large pasture in half, its waters flowing to the river. Over the years, the creek has eroded the soil and carved a deep gash in the land.

The sandy walls of this small canyon are four or five feet high. One day Lupus discovers ducks occupying this creek where the eroded walls are the steepest.

For five consecutive days after making this discovery, he dashes down the hill and across the field to plunge into the creek from the highest point on its bank. He duplicates this pattern each day: Lupus leaps into the creek, and the ducks, honking in panic, suddenly depart, rising close to the high bank as they escape, apparently never in any real danger. After five days of this apparently pointless exercise, I am both amused and embarrassed by the futility of Lupus's shenanigans. As far as I'm concerned, he has no hope of catching a duck. He simply soars into the cold water of the creek again and again, and again and again comes up empty-handed. I shake my head. Lupus is very bright and alert most of the time. This mad dash across the pasture, ending with a resounding splash and the loud honking of the ducks, seems uncharacteristically stupid for a creature with his intelligence.

It's on the sixth day that I learn I am wrong, and why I'm wrong.

On the sixth day, it all begins the same way. Even knowing how Lupus's mad dash across the field will turn out, how futile it will be, I still feel compelled to watch it take place, his blinding speed, his canny silence. As I observe the scene this time, however, I am staggered by what he does. This time, instead of leaping into the creek when he reaches the highest point on the bank, he changes direction and soars into the air at a sharp right angle. The ducks, now trained to depart the creek in the same frightened manner each day, fly out of the water and begin to climb towards this high section of bank. As Lupus leaps several feet into the air, he narrowly misses snatching one of them out of its pattern of flight. It is an extremely near miss, from my vantage point less than a foot. And I realize for the first time that day how patiently Lupus will set his traps when he is on a hunt.

On the seventh day, and on every day after that, he leaves the ducks alone. He sprung his trap and failed, although barely. Still, it didn't work, and he doesn't try it again.

A black squirrel chatters from a tree branch several hundred yards from our house. It's early afternoon, and Lupus and I are returning from our sojourn through the woods.

Lupus stops to survey the squirrel that is giving him so much lip.

"C'mon, Loop. Let's go," I say.

But he ignores me. Instead he casually walks into a thick stand of shrubs at the base of the tree.

"C'mon, Loop."

It's as if I'm not there at all. He doesn't move, he remains entirely rigid. Although he has been panting with the heat of this late spring day, he has given this up for the moment and transformed himself into a statue. A slight breeze tousles his fur, but beyond this slight movement he might just as well be carved from stone.

I would call to him again, I want to take him home for a drink of water, but I notice that the squirrel, having now forgotten about Lupus, has begun to descend the tree. I cannot help myself, I must watch the proceedings unfold. In a few moments, stupid and forgetful, the squirrel falls into the trap.

One moment Lupus is absolutely still, the next he has pounced with blazing speed on his victim. To my displeasure, it takes him only an instant to snap the squirrel's neck. To my horror, he then decides to eat it. My vocal objections go entirely unheeded. I know about the strength in Lupus's jaws, how tightly he can lock them and how sharp his teeth are. I would be a fool to try to wrest the squirrel from him.

About this time, I begin to discuss with my partner the merits of moving to western Canada to begin all over again. I cannot stay here, I say, withering in my defeat, waiting for something good to happen. I have been approached by another area newspaper to sell my own newspaper's name, which is virtually all I have left he can buy. He isn't offering a great deal of money, but it will pay off some of my personal debts, and there will be enough left over to get us out west to begin again.

But my partner demurs. We've debated this subject — me wanting to move to the mountains, her wanting to stay in Ontario — before, nearly five years ago, prior to the newspaper project when our relationship was newer and our financial circumstances were much different than they are now. Except for the economic desperation now surrounding us, the arguments remain the same. This time, though, if the sale of the newspaper's name works out, I promise myself I will not change my mind. Besides, I continue to believe that if I go to the Rockies she will eventually join me there.

Lupus often comes up in our discussions. We both love him. He is like our matrimonial child. She decides that he should go with me, not because I have more right to him than she does, but because she sees a similarity between us that continues to develop. I sense that she is right, although I am still discovering what we have in common. One thing is clear, however: Lupus does not frighten me the way he has frightened her, on those occasions when he has been stubbornly playful.

I remember one winter's morning about a month after the newspaper's collapse. The three of us were outside, walking in the deep snow. Wanting to wrestle with her, he grabbed the hem of her long coat. To her dismay, he easily pulled her to the ground. When she showed her fear, I interceded, noticing the power with which he locked his jaws. But he soon let go because I was not frightened of him. My partner's fear was not Lupus's intention—he merely wanted to play. What frightened her, it was clear, was his physical strength and speed. It was this, rather than any malevolence, that would have caused her injury.

That July, as the sale of the newspaper's name is negotiated, we debate several times what to do. Although I do not realize it as clearly as my partner does, she and I are continuing to move apart; the mesh of our shared goals is coming undone. We have different ideas of how to save ourselves, how to reclaim our respective lives. Love has nothing to do with this process. The "us" in our relationship is giving way to the necessary "me" and "you."

Early that summer, as it becomes more likely I will camp my way out west, I erect the tent in our front yard, to try it out, and to figure out what else I might need to take with me. Also,

I want to know how Lupus will behave sharing such a small residence with me.

I take great pains with this experiment. I select a balmy July night and coax Lupus into the tent. He seems unperturbed, and I crawl into my sleeping bag prepared to read a while before turning out the lantern, which I have placed just outside the tent. But Lupus is restless. He stands at the mesh, gazing outside, not wanting to lie down on his blanket. I wonder if he needs to urinate. I unzip the mesh, and he slips outside. I go back to my book. Several minutes pass before I remember to call him back inside. Gently I call out—it is very late now and the nearby household is asleep—but he does not respond. Annoyed, I leave the tent to look for him. Although the property shimmers in a generous wash of moonlight, there is no sign of him. Not wanting to wake everyone, and not wanting to search the fields or woods for him in the darkness, I return to the tent so that I might be there when he comes back. After a while, I fall into fitful sleep.

When I awake the next morning, I discover that Lupus has not returned. The rest of that day is lost to tears and angst and searching. Several times my partner and I patrol the roads all around our home in an ever-increasing radius. I already know how much ground Lupus can cover in very little time. We have alerted our neighbours and have called the local radio stations. They have kindly placed a bulletin on the air. Separately and in tandem, we spend hours on foot in the fields and woods with which Lupus is familiar. But mostly we patrol in the car, systematically exploring an ever-expanding grid of country and town roads, hoping we'll catch a glimpse of him. The longer he is lost to us, the further away from us he has likely travelled. During our final daylight drive along the various sideroads in the area, we fall into greater despair. Lupus has been gone for more than sixteen hours.

My partner and I speculate out loud about the various unhappy scenarios that might have befallen Lupus. Hit by a vehicle on a road we haven't covered. Shot by a farmer some distance from where we live. Picked up by a passing motorist attracted to his appearance and vitality. Lost in the woods where, strangely enough, he sometimes seems to belong.

That evening, as we weep and repeatedly go over these various possibilities, our telephone rings in response to a public service notice on a local radio station. Afraid to hope, as humans are when they are feeling pain, we drive down the highway to a farm less than a mile away. Lupus has been there all day long while we were combing a large geography elsewhere, looking for him. He has befriended a couple of hounds and, to the farmer's amusement and ours, one of his lambs. Lupus and the lamb have played together several times that day. My astonishment at his choice of playmates overcomes my relief that he didn't kill or injure the lamb, which is what one might reasonably expect.

When my partner and I arrive, Lupus darts towards us, glad to see us. Then, several yards from us and our car, he halts and reconsiders. He wants to stay here with his friends. I can see he isn't ready to come home yet, if at all. As I advance on him, carrying his leash, he enters a nearby dog house and disappears from view. The dog house is large and, in the dusk, I cannot see him. I must reach inside, not really certain how adamant he is about his refusal to leave, to connect the leash to his chain collar. It takes a few moments to accomplish this task by touch, but Lupus does not object. When he is connected, I tug and verbally cajole him out of the dog house. After this, he accepts his fate. He waits patiently enough in our car while we conduct our rituals of gratitude and apology to the people who have hosted him for nearly twenty-four hours.

A couple of days later, on a hot, muggy, extremely windy day, a gust knocks in the screen on our living room window. My partner and I return from a short trip into the city to discover that Lupus is gone again, having leaped through the opening where the screen had been. This time it is obvious where I should begin my search. Apologizing profusely, explaining about the window screen and the high winds that allowed Lupus to effect his unorthodox escape, I must once again retrieve him from the same farm and get him into the car.

This time Lupus's host issues a warning. He says Lupus looks like a wolf, especially from a distance. He says another farmer who doesn't know him is likely to shoot him. Soberly I nod. I agree that I must take extra care to keep him safely on our own property. As I drive home with him it strikes me quite clearly that on farms this close to the city we are both out of our element. When we go west in a month's time to the Rocky Mountain wilderness, we are likely to find the place where we both belong.

Lupus, I will eventually learn, does not get fleas. Even a couple of years from now, when Charlie the cat suffers fleas, they will shun Lupus. I will learn that the old adage — that fleas are a cat's revenge on dogs — does not apply to him. Still, Lupus's visit to the farm down the highway is not without its pestilent price. A tick burrows a home inside his tail. It's not the tick that is the problem, but the ferocity with which Lupus removes it from his flesh. Lupus bites the tick out of his tail so viciously that he tears out a large clump of fur and flesh, leaving himself bleeding. A few days later, I discover the wound is badly infected. I have already arranged to take him to the vet a few miles away, for his rabies shot and heartworm medication. Now we must also deal with the obviously painful infection in the wound on his tail.

I've known this vet for some time. He is an accomplished professional. He recognizes the wolf in Lupus and is quite taken with him. He even calls to a young associate to come into the examination room to see him.

"Come in here," he says, "and have a look at our cousin from the wild."

It is the first clue I have that Lupus might be more wolf than I had previously believed.

It takes all three of us to hold him still while the infected wound is treated. Even so, pound for pound, Lupus is so strong we can barely restrain him while the vet shaves his tail and scrapes off the scab to treat the wound with disinfectant. In the end, Lupus wraps his jaws around my arm for comfort while he endures the pain. I trust him. I let him do this as my way of showing caring and empathy.

"Amazing," the vet proclaims when we are done. "The way he held onto your arm and didn't bite down."

"What you were doing must have hurt," I conjecture.

"You bet it did," he says.

Lupus's wound heals quickly. It takes a couple of months, however, for the fur that was shaved away to grow back. For several weeks, he wears the scar of what has happened to him.

I remain naive about the changes I will soon go through, of course. I believe the process of recovery — from the debacle of the newspaper, from my own abuse of my health, from the psychological motivation that led me to behave the way I did — will occur painlessly. In this I am wrong. The need to drive oneself has a sameness about it, and we derive comfort from familiarity. But change is unfamiliar; it tends to frighten us. We resist it because we fear having to face the unknown armed with only our faith in ourselves. My changes will not be painless; I will have to find the strength to break the bonds of familiarity, to give up habits that feel right only because I am used to them.

The last few weeks before the drive out west are fretful and turbulent for me. I fear my partner will not join me when I find a place for us. I fear I will not discover a new location where I can make myself acceptable again. I suppose I fear being alone. When I am alone, I will have to decide what is best for me. I will have to learn to be confident that the private person I am is authentically me. My spiritual impoverishment, my denial of who I am, has taken decades to develop. Even with Lupus here to encourage me, it is going to take some time to tear down such a strong and formidable wall, I suspect. I have no idea that we are only just beginning, that it will, in fact, take a very long time.

And the terrible irony is that one must go through this kind of transformation before one is able to understand the need for it. We only realize what we need to go through after we have finally managed to do it. Understanding doesn't come from the act of transformation itself, but lies in our knowledge of what we required transformation *from*.

December 1992

I am told occasionally by people entering the newspaper office that I stagger when I walk. I have acquired the gait of a much older man. I feel used up by the endless fatigue. I do not sleep much and my physical coordination testifies to this.

The newspaper is published on Wednesdays. I write virtually all of it myself, covering as many newsworthy community meetings and events as I can squeeze into a workweek. I work Saturdays and Sundays, usually from nine in the morning until one the next morning. On Mondays, I begin at nine a.m. and continue working until two a.m. on Wednesday. On Wednesdays, I am up again at five a.m. to see to the paper's distribution.

The rest of the week is spent covering local events, chasing accounts, and coming up with schemes to increase advertising sales. So it goes week after week.

It's now December. When Christmas arrives, I will close the office until New Year's. This is the only vacation I take each year, and it's a business decision. The newspaper makes no money over the Christmas holidays, so it is more productive to shut the office during this period. Yet during this time off I am restless and disoriented. This one week off is not a vacation but a period of vulnerability. I feel subject to an indefinable anxiety, predicated upon economic worries and a mindset more attuned to the frantic pace of the other fifty-one weeks in the year. I don't know how to relax. I'm afraid that if I stop pushing myself for even a moment something malevolent and ugly will catch me and tear me to pieces.

I shouldn't feel this way: the business I run is a successful one, at least on paper. It runs consistently in the black, it is popular, and when I visit our network of newsstands to deliver the latest edition, there is rarely even a single copy of the old edition left to take back. In the past six months, I have picked up only two or three copies that have not been sought out by loyal readers. A municipal survey revealed that our newspaper is overwhelmingly the favoured source for information about community events or developments.

But the country has been manipulated into another recession. Accounts are slow to be paid, and my personal anxiety now hinges exclusively on the money we are owed. At times, unpaid accounts represent one-fifth of our annual sales.

My bank, like every bank, is a fair-weather friend. During periods of economic uncertainty, it has called in eighty percent of my line of operating credit, quintupled my service charges, and adjusted my interest rate from one and a half over prime to six and a half over prime. I have survived all of these violations, but they have cost me dearly. I've tried to change banks, but new banks do not want my business. They are aware of my constant need to chase accounts, aware that much of the newspaper's success hinges on my personal efforts. They do not wish to take on the risk.

And my office has become my residence. I have put a small refrigerator and microwave in a corner so that I can prepare and eat food there. There is a couch nearby, which I sometimes lie down on. I don't sleep. I just lie on my back, my hands laced over my heaving chest, fighting a periodic trembling in my hands, trying to fathom the exhausted stagger in my walk that has made me an old man at forty-four years of age.

But I am about to meet Lupus for the first time.

My partner encounters him first. Once a week or so, she drops in at the animal shelter while driving about the city soliciting advertising. Although we share a love of animals, we do not share this pastime. For me, looking at animals in cages and knowing I cannot save them is subtle torture. Should I ever succumb to the urge to rescue one of them, I know that my work schedule would not allow me the hours necessary to take care of my new charge. However, following one of her visits to the animal shelter, my partner tells me about a dog she has seen. She has been told that it is a Siberian husky, but the attendant at the shelter thinks there is some wolf mixed in. My partner wants me to go and have a look at this animal. I remind her that neither of us has the time right now to take care of a pet.

But she goes to see him again that December and tells me how beautiful he is. Again, she asks me to visit him. Although I doubt I'll ever find the time, and I haven't changed my mind about the impracticality of getting a dog, I tell her I'll see what I can do.

In truth, I have little intention of visiting the animal shelter. But one afternoon, while driving back to the office from a meeting with a client, I succumb to impulse and drive through the shelter's ramshackle gates. I park the car, step out into the cold, rutted snow, and stand there for a moment, wondering what I'm doing in this place. I do not feel comfortable here, preparing to take a few minutes of my day on a dubious mission unrelated to work or economic survival.

I nearly get back into my car, then, for no reason I'm aware of, I decide to go in. I cross the parking lot and enter the animal shelter. Inside I explain that I wish to see a particular dog. No one volunteers to accompany me. Instead I am given directions and have to find my own way through a network of caged cats and down the various hallways to where the dogs are kept. I am greeted by a loud cacophony of barks, whines, and excited yips. The air smells of urine and dog shit, of dry dog food and damp fur. The noise takes some getting used to; it's been years since I visited an animal shelter.

The husky isn't hard to find. He's in the third cage from the end, surrounded on either side by baying hounds of various breeds. My partner is right: he is an extremely handsome fellow. He's a little smaller than I expected, the height of a Siberian husky but thinner. The typical Siberian tends towards muscular stockiness. I glance up at a cardboard sign above the door of his cage: *Siberian husky/wolf,* it says, the word "wolf" with a single line drawn through it as if the word was written in error.

Amid all the whining, barking, growling, and tail-wagging, this dog remains silent and still. The hounds in the cages nearby snarl at him periodically as they pace back and forth, but he ignores this entirely. He does not respond in any way. His tail does not wag. He is as aloof as he can be. I crouch in front of the door of his cage and wait for him to notice me, to evince the slightest interest that I have come to meet him. He drinks some water, calmly, delicately. All around us, dogs cry out, throw themselves against their cages. The husky remains silent. At last, however, he looks at me.

"Hello, big guy," I say.

He does not approach the door to be touched. Still five feet from me, he calmly sits down on the concrete floor to stare me down.

"You're a handsome fellow, aren't you?" I say. He simply gazes at me. "The point is, how did you end up in a place like this?"

His head tilts back, and he howls. While not a bone-chiller, his howl has a loud authority. For a moment, the other dogs in the kennel fall silent. A moment later, when Lupus does not howl again, the dogs renew their gibberish, and everything returns to normal.

Back at the shelter's main counter, I ask if anyone has expressed interest in the Siberian husky. They tell me that deposits have been put down twice on him. In both cases, though, the depositors have had a change of heart and not shown up to claim him. I am surprised by this. The deposit is half the cost of the animal.

When they ask if I am interested in taking him, I demur, explaining the long hours I work and the inconvenience he might represent.

"He's a handsome fellow," I say. They agree with me, but they've grown reserved now that I've confessed my ambivalence. I ask them not to destroy him. I leave my name and telephone number, requesting that they let me know if no one wants him before his allotted time is up. They assure me that they'll call.

Outside I am overcome by a sudden, inexplicable sadness. Fatigue, perhaps. Or seeing myself in a cage of a different sort than those inside the Humane Society. Whatever the reason, it is several hours before I can get the image of the husky in his cage out of my mind.

My partner takes matters into her own hands a few days later. As a birthday present to herself, she visits the shelter again and puts down a deposit on him. Then she calls me to tell me what she's done. I sigh, giving in. The reasons I was resistant remain, but she has every right to make this choice on her own.

"We might just as well get him then," I say. "The deposit is half the cost."

"Do you have any money?" she asks.

"I'll have to borrow it from petty cash."

We meet to pick him up a couple of hours later, after we've closed the office for the day. For once, I have no meeting to attend, no event to cover. I can retreat to an evening at home.

There's paperwork to do at the shelter's front counter first, and we purchase a leash. He's been neutered and had his shots, we're told. As we wait for him to join us, I clearly recall his aloofness from my earlier visit. I can imagine his indignation at the medical procedures he's been through. I sense that, after they were over, he was probably insulted.

We announce that we've already decided to call him Lupus, but our news elicits little response. The animal shelter people still want to resist any acknowledgment of the part of him that might be wild. It won't be long before shelters such as this one adopt a policy against taking in animals that are part wolf.

Lupus enters the shelter's foyer on the leash we've just purchased. His ears are back, expressing his resignation and irritation. Then, with little warning, he squats and defecates on the floor. Strangely enough, I assume some kind of responsibility for his action — he's ours now and we're answerable for his behaviour — and I hear myself apologize. Already I have something else to apologize for. At first I assumed that his shitting on the floor was just nervousness, but when I glance at him his face is indignant, even defiant. He's like a departing hotel guest who has found a disagreeable way to complain about the establishment's lousy service. I sense his cockiness.

I see little fear in him, little need to apologize the way I so often do. He will crouch in fear a few times over the next week, however, as I am affixing the chain leash I will buy to replace the canvas one he's connected to now. I will arrive at the conclusion that someone has tried to discipline him by striking him with such a leash. But after a week or so, when he concludes this kind of abuse will never occur again, he will learn to appreciate the leash as an announcement that he is going for a walk. He will approach me confidently when he sees it in my hands.

For the moment, I am assured that his biological complaint is not upsetting for the animal shelter staff, but we're now informed that Lupus isn't house-trained, that he's never stayed indoors. Privately I fret that house-training an adult dog will be difficult, especially in view of how busy we are. I do not yet know that Lupus will be house-trained in less than twenty-four hours. Doing his business outside will clearly be his preference.

We must stop at the grocery store near the newspaper office to purchase some dog food and other pet supplies. On the way, glancing into the back seat at him, I notice him clutch a length of seatbelt in his jaws. Before I can pull over to take it away from him, he literally rips the seatbelt in two. I am astonished by this act—not by the vandalism behind it, but by the strength and sharpness of his jaws and teeth. I realize the flimsy red leash we have purchased at the animal shelter will not do the job. I must buy a chain leash and collar, and I will have to make these purchases soon, whether I can afford them or not.

In our home, we let him wander from room to room, exploring his new surroundings. He tours the house calmly and only once, returning to the kitchen shortly afterwards to lie down. Our gazes meet. "I guess it'll do," his expression says. If Lupus could shrug indifferently, I sense he would choose to do so at this moment.

"This guy doesn't lack for self-esteem," I remark, more or less to myself. My partner later confesses to making the same observation herself.

Later that night, I sit on the edge of the bed, untying the sneakers I wear whenever I am inside the house. I'm very tired, and I want to retire for the night. My partner is in the adjoining bathroom, readying herself for bed. Lupus enters the bedroom and gazes at what I am doing. He approaches, crouches, and insinuates himself between my calves and the side of the bed. Surprised at this display of affection from an animal who has, until now, been so cocky and aloof, I let go of the shoelaces to reach down and stroke him. Suddenly, with astonishing speed, he jerks upwards against my knees. I grunt in astonishment as the force of the blow flips me backwards onto the bed. A moment later, our gazes lock. Then, as calmly as he entered, Lupus trots out of the room.

I discover that I am grinning. I chuckle to myself. And it occurs to me how long it's been since I have smiled.

Epilogue

In 2001 a colleague in Muskoka reported encountering a female husky chained to a tree on rural, wooded property he was considering buying. The dog had food, and there was snow to quench her thirst, and she didn't seem otherwise abused in any way, but on the frozen lake not far away he noticed an assortment of tracks in the snow. Wolves, he said. The husky, helplessly chained to the tree, was terrified. I believe the dog might have been there to be mated to a wolf.

The cavalier abuse of this poor husky explains why I say no whenever people ask me if I would replace Lupus with another husky-wolf cross. In view of the reverence and affection I still feel for Lupus, people tend to be surprised by my answer. If they're interested, I explain.

Lupus taught me to be an individual, to be the person I really am, to resist the powerful forces in society that would supplant my personal reality with some version of their own. Breeding wolves with dogs, I feel, is indicative of a similar kind of suppression or interference. It's unfair to dogs, who have found, generally speaking, a happy place and a role in conventional human society. It's unfair to wolves, who need freedom and their own society to live their lives with purpose. To try to knit these two disparate worlds together is improper and unkind. Neither dogs nor wolves have the intellectual capacity to deal with the existential crisis that results. Resolution of this kind of crisis should be left to human beings, who have the capacity to succeed or fail at it.

What's wild is wild, what's domestic is domestic. Sometimes in humans, too.

There's another reason I believe Lupus cannot be replaced: our relationship was unique, probably an aberration. Lupus clearly possessed a wild streak, but I had an uncommon patience with his wildness, due in part to my circumstances at the time. Also, although he didn't always behave like a dog, he was unusually gentle most of the time and this, too, was extraordinary good fortune. It is rare that a partially wild animal does not display a viciousness that can lead to disaster. Lupus and I, however, enjoyed a patient affection for one another from which the seeds of our friendship sprung. A more typical dog owner and a more typical wolf-cross living inside the many rules of conventional society, in a collision between wild and tame expectations, might not have fared so well.

And so I do not even contemplate trying to replace Lupus. It would not only be wrong or cruel or potentially disastrous, it would represent pointless hypocrisy. It would negate all I believe I learned from him.

But I still miss him. The side of my nature I have learned must remain untamed, by conventional standards at least, is the side that misses him most. It's the cocky half of me, the half with so much self-esteem, the half that occasionally howls at the moon. When the pressure to conform to conventional minutiae is vaguely tempting because of its enticing familiarity, I miss his courage and independence. I miss the way he would not heel. I miss the inspiration I took from this, the reality about myself I learned to see reflected in Lupus's mirror.

Mingus, Lupus's best canine friend, could be still alive, as far as I know. I am no longer associated with his master and I haven't seen Mingus in years. I have a photo of Mingus and me hung on my living room wall that was taken a few weeks after Lupus died. Mingus seems vaguely comforting in this photograph, while I still slouch in grief, grey and sad with loss. We love our animals; they love us. This love succeeds in simple ways. I find such simple, undemanding love more difficult to achieve when I am dealing with humans. Not impossible. But difficult.

One autumn afternoon a few years ago, I scattered Lupus's ashes in Algonquin Park, along a walking trail at the edge of some rushing water. The trail, called Whiskey Rapids, is reputably a place where wolves sometimes gather. I thought he would be happy there. Some of the bone and ash drifted near the surface of the rapids, away from where I stood. I watched it float away from me. Some of the heavier particles sank into little pools where the rapids were forming themselves. I wept a little that day. Giving a friend back to the place where he began is a cruelly ambivalent act—we don't want to let them go, yet we know there's nothing physical to keep.

Still, I speak of him often to people, and sometimes regale them with stories. I forget little about who Lupus was. I push on without him, because he would expect this of me. This is part of what made Lupus such a good friend. He sensed who I really am even when I didn't know myself.

Or if I knew, I didn't have the courage then to stay my own course.

What would Lupus do? I unwittingly ask myself when faced with an important choice. Even now, years later, I sometimes find myself wondering what his answer would be.

Acknowledgments

There are people to thank with respect to the writing of *Every Wolf's Howl*. Sue Sumeraj was an early enthusiast for the project. The people at Freehand Books have been wonderful to work with. My deepest thanks goes to Robyn Read, who acquired this book, edited it with extreme sensitivity, and continues to champion it. My wife, Jennifer Rouse Barbeau, has read this work and discussed various aspects of it with me on too many occasions to mention, for which I am deeply indebted to her. Her support is invaluable to me.

Barry Grills' stories have appeared in numerous literary journals and magazines, including *Quarry, Grain,* and the *University of Windsor Review,* as well as various anthologies, including *Best Canadian Stories.* He is also the author of three cultural biographies from Quarry Press on the lives of Anne Murray, Alanis Morissette, and Celine Dion, as well as an updated Celine Dion biography, co-authored with Jim Brown. He is a past chair of The Writers' Union of Canada and the Book and Periodical Council, and he has been both a federal election candidate and a municipal councillor. He currently lives in North Bay, Ontario.